DIVORCE, REMARRIAGE AND BLENDED FAMILIES:

DIVORCE COUNSELING AND RESEARCH PERSPECTIVES

by

Christopher J. Pino, Ph.D.

Authors Choice Press

San Jose New York Lincoln Shanghai

Divorce, Remarriage, and Blended Families
Divorce Counseling and Research Perspectives 2nd Edition

Authors Choice Press
an imprint of iUniverse.com, Inc.

For information address:
iUniverse.com, Inc.
5220 S 16th, Ste. 200
Lincoln, NE 68512
www.iuniverse.com

Originally published by R & E Research

ISBN: 0-595-16858-2

Printed in the United States of America

DEDICATION

To my wonderful parents, and
loving wife who encourage me
greatly.

ACKNOWLEDGMENTS

Chapter III, THE MARITAL AUTOPSY, reprinted by permission of Haworth Press. It originally appeared in *Journal of Divorce*, Vol. 4, Issue No. 1, Fall, 1980.

Chapter V, DIVORCE ADJUSTMENT RESEARCH, is reprinted by permission of Pilgrimage Press, Inc. It originally appeared (as "Divorce Imagery, Post-Divorce Coping, and Assertiveness") in *Journal of Counseling & Psychotherapy*, Vol. IV, No. 1, 1981.

Chapter VII, REMARRIAGE AND BLENDED FAMILIES, is reprinted by permission of Brigham Young University Press. It originally appeared in *Family Perspective*, Spring, 1981, Vol. 15, No. 2.

TABLE OF CONTENTS

Page

PREFACE

This book was written in order to provide practitioners (e.g., divorce counselors) and students of divorce with a coherent set of reviews and research on divorce adjustment and remarriage. Chapter I sets forth the social and psychological parameters of divorce. Chapters II and III report on analyzing the demise of marriage. This is patterned after the psychological autopsy, widely used in suicidology. The next chapter, Chapter IV, presents an overview of divorce counseling methods, with case material illustrating clinical use of the marital autopsy. In Chapter V, divorce adjustment research on a non-clinical sample is discussed.

Chapters VII and VIII are organized around a survey of remarried individuals. This work describes the process of forming a blended family. The last chapter summarizes the contributions of the book and outlines some prominent positions regarding divorce policy. Highlighted is the government's role in providing landmark legislation to aid single parent families to cope in a two parent family world.

CHAPTER I

SOCIAL AND PSYCHOLOGICAL FACTORS IN DIVORCE

INTRODUCTION

The increasing divorce rate over the last generation has spurred major changes in our culture. Jessie Bernard for instance has talked about the new family life style (1975). Carl Rogers (1972) in his book, *Becoming Partners: Marriage and its Alternatives*, gives another illustration of the variety of alternatives that are concomitant to the cultural changes associated with divorce. The literature now abounds with information on every aspect of divorce and thus the focus of this chapter will be on the social and psychological factors of divorce.

This volume reports a three-phase study of divorce adjustment and remarriage. Phase One analyzes facets of the decline of marriage and the divorce process by using the Psychological Autopsy Method (here renamed "Marital Autopsy"). Specific rating measures were taken in a divorce counseling group and were compared with married and unmarried adults in counseling in order to more fully understand how these individuals lives differed from non-divorced subjects. All subjects were drawn from the same clinical sample. Such comparisons of clinical subjects are uncommon and can fill needed gaps in our existing knowledge of the divorce process. Also, the Marital Autopsy can be easily adapted as a useful clinical tool. Case examples of this are presented in Chapter IV.

Phase Two developed a model for predicting divorce adjustment by confirming Holmes & Rahe's (1976) Life-Stress Theory and Nye's (1977) Resource Theory. The research used the same population to test the theory by a statistical procedure known as path analysis. This comprehensive theory has important clinical application (as discussed in Chapter V) and policy applications (as discussed in Chapter VII).

Phase Three of the study investigates the divorced counseling subjects three (3) years after divorce by use of follow-up survey. These individuals who remarried were compared with remarried individuals who attended divorce support groups and a third group who has not received either treatment. Thus, the effect of treatment was assessed, as well as several factors of step-family adjustment in three comparative groups. This research has important implications for therapy and educational programming in divorce adjustment and remarriage preparation (as discussed in Chapter VII).

Chapter II will present the methodologies of all three phases. Chapter III will present results of Phase One of the research; Chapter V will give the results of Phase Two,[1] and Phase Three will be provided by Chapter VII.

BACKGROUND

In analyzing the statistics on divorce in the United States, our records have only been available for a little over a century.

Around 1860 there were fewer than 8,000 divorces; in 1940—264,000; in 1950—385,000; in 1974—970,000. In September, 1979, there were an estimated 93,000 divorces granted in the United States with the rate being 5:1 per one thousand population (*Marriage and Divorce Today*, December 31, 1979). It must also be noted that there is also an upward trend in marriages continuing throughout 1979 so as divorce is thriving, so is marriage.

GEOGRAPHIC AREAS

Wars have tended to be followed by increases in divorce rates in the United States. This was true particularly for the Civil War, World Wars I and II, and the Vietnamese Conflict. Leslie (1976) reports that in 1970 in the United States there was one divorce for every three marriages. It is also noteworthy that the long run trend in divorce rates tends to vary as does a business cycle according to Goode (1961).

Leslie (1976) notes that urban regions tend to have higher rates of divorce. Divorce rates appear to have regional trends with the West having the highest rates, then the South, then the North Central, and finally the Northeast region of the United States. This may have something to do with geographic distribution of people according to religious affiliation. For example, Roman Catholics who tend to have lower divorce rates (but a higher rate of desertion) are particularly over-represented in the Northern and Eastern sections of the country.

RACE

There are variations according to race: for example, in

1971 census figures reveal that there was a 2.8% rate for white males, 3.4% for non-white males, 3.8% for white females and 5.6% for non-white females.

ECONOMIC FACTORS

Goode (1961) reported that divorce was related to occupational status with upper occupational levels having lower rates and the rates increasing as we descend the occupational, educational and socioeconomic level. Similar results were found by Hillman (1962). The number of children affected by divorce has increased, as has the proportion of divorce involving children. These figures have begun to plateau recently, however, as family size has begun to decrease.

REASONS FOR DIVORCE

The major source of complaints leading to the termination of a marriage are: incompatibility, adultery, barrenness or sterility, impotence or frigidity, economic incapacity or non-support, cruelty and quarrelsomeness or nagging (Barrelson and Steiner, 1964). Actual legal grounds have varied from state to state, but overall about 52% of U.S. divorces were granted based on grounds of either physical or emotional cruelty. Twenty-three percent of U.S. divorces were granted on the grounds of desertion, and non-support accounted for 4%, adultery about 1% (Glick and Carter, 1970). As more states have enacted no-fault divorce, these figures are beginning to change.

Goode (1961) lists the following factors as related to greater proneness to divorce: marrying at a young age (15 to 19 years), a short engagement or no engagement, non-attendance at

4

church or mixed faith marriages, short acquaintanceship before marriage, couples whose parents had unhappy marriages, general dissimilarity in the background of spouses, disapproval by kin or friends of the marriage, and different definitions of a husband and wife as to their mutual role obligations.

Practical considerations along economic lines, related to divorce are clearly pointed out by Furstenburg (1976). The high rate of divorced in those marrying young can be mainly accounted for by premarital pregnancy. This inflicts economic hardship and curtails the normal preparation for marriage in the engagement process. Furstenburg points to the particularly distressful situation young black couples in this category may have because of the added disadvantage of social and economic discrimination. Other economic considerations are presented by Chevlin (1979) who noted that stable employment for males is associated with lower divorce rates. However, females who have potential wages similar to that of their spouses have higher divorce rates. This widens their range of options, thus increasing the desirability of divorce.

INTERPERSONAL ASPECTS

Mueller and Pope (1977) have discussed the transmission of marital instability between generations. Their study indicated that mate selection tended to create high risk circumstances in that children of divorce tend to marry early and limit educational possibilities. This would certainly show an immaturity that would make communication and bargaining difficult to these marriages. Nye and McLaughlin (1977) have utilized a resource theory to predict marital satisfaction and success. The theory predicted quite well for women. Their satisfaction in marriage was based on the role competence of their husbands in the areas of therapeutic (companionship), and child socialization.

5

In contrast, the economic provider and sexual roles of men were, for the most part, taken for granted. Trying to predict marital satisfaction of the husbands was a great deal more complex and difficult. The authors clarified the role between marital dissatisfaction as directly related to marital dissolution. That being that high expectations for reciprocity in the mate's marital functioning creates a situation where the spouse feels cheated and willing to move away from the marriage. The ability to follow through with divorce is also dependent, as Scanzoni (1979) relates, to economic factors. He found that in marriage "money is power," inasmuch as women's increased earning power is associated with a tendency to higher divorce rates. Because she has higher bargaining power, her dependency on her partner is reduced and she is more likely to see divorce as a positive step in her life.

Levinger's (1979) social psychological analysis of marital dissolution investigated the costs and rewards associated with marriage. These constitute an attraction in marriage in the following three categories:

1. Material rewards.

2. Symbolic rewards (status).

3. Similarity between mates and the affectional rewards (e.g., recreation, companionship, sexual enjoyment).

Therefore, the desire for divorce can be seen as a situation when the cost of the marriage exceeds the rewards. The divorce may seem a particularly likely attraction when the alternatives to marriage seem good. Hence, the possiblity for financial and emotional independence, self-actualization, and other sources of affection (for instance, a preferred sex partner, or the possibility of moving closer to their kins whom their spouse has always disliked) prove to be important factors.

PERSONALITY FACTORS

Individual personality traits and types of psychopathology play an important role in marital, as well as divorce, adjustment. Indeed, these factors play an important role in getting married in the first place.

Framo (1974) suggested that the reasons for marriage are also the reasons for divorce, inasmuch as there are "hidden agendas" that are seldom voiced during the mating process. These have to do with unfilled needs, the possibility of mastering an old conflict, or possibly even self-punishment. Therefore, a person may marry someone they feel is an improvement on their family of origin, or who will help them to escape the family situation that they find problematic. Unfortunately, this romantic love and the courtship in their engagement process often serves to be a set of "blinders." Later, after the honeymoon phase, as the marriage life cycle has occurred, the person realizes that their needs have not been met by their mate and feels cheated and ready to dissolve the marriage. Life span theorists (Gould, 1972; Sheey, 1978) points to the early 30's in life as a time when individuals reflect upon their lives and search for new beginnings. Part of their search may be in finding fault in their own marriage and moving away from it whether emotionally or through actual divorce or separation as a way to better their own lives.

Bergler (1948) in his provocative book *Divorce Won't Help* sees masochistic neurotic tendencies creating difficulties for people in their marriage. Blaming the marriage does not constitute an effective solution, nor does divorce, to what he feels is a personal problem.

7

STAGES OF DIVORCE

There are several theories of stages of divorce which will be presented here as a backdrop to the Marital Autopsy scheme utilized in the present presearch.

Herman (1974) describes divorce as a grief process. Utilizing Kubler-Ross' theory on *Death and Dying,* she sees divorce as similar to the stages in the dying process which are: denial, anger, bargaining, depression, and finally acceptance. Another idea about stages in divorce is promulgated by Bohannan (1974). He sees divorce as a series of stages which involve six steps (not always in the order presented): emotional divorce, legal divorce, financial divorce, co-parental divorce, community divorce, and psychic divorce. Emotional divorce can take place without an actual legal process and many people may maintain their marriage despite feeling a "death of love" for their mate. Legal divorce only begins a period of detachment which involves the division of financial resources, the termination of the dual parent household, the possible estrangement of friends (as in "community divorce"), and the final emotional independence as seen in the sixth stage of the divorce process.

Kessler (1977) has a seven stage theory of divorce. Kessler's stages of divorce are as follows:

1. Beginning in the disillusionment stage of marriage after the "honeymoon" period ends;

2. Erosion period where dissatisfaction occurs (and sexual alliances may occur as well);

3. Detachment, or emotional divorce period;

4. Physical separation stage;

5.   Mourning period;

6.   Second adolescence; and

7.   Exploration and hard work phase, a time to prepare for a new life which may likely include remarriage.

She has developed therapy strategies to match each stage of divorce adjustment.

Garfield (1979) sees four issues as pertinent to readjustment after divorce. This involves the ability:

1.   To become emotionally separated from a spouse;

2.   To become an individual in the period following marital separation;

3.   To achieve a degree of rebalance to relationships with family-of-origin members (this means the family members acceptance of the divorce and perhaps of the new partner as significant in determining the success of the marriage as seen in Bernard's (1971) research);

4.   The ability to become integrated in a new life style which may include remarriage.

OUTCOMES OF DIVORCE

Weiss (1976) discussed the impact of separation on individuals. He noted that individuals that separate may vary in mood from deep depression (usually accompanied by a lessened self-esteem), to euphoria (accompanied by increased self-confidence).

What seems to be common is the alternation or shift of moods, from his research. Bloom, White and Asher (1978) describe divorce as a stressful life event. They quote higher admission rates into psychiatric facilities, increased motor vehicle accidents, increased disease morbidity, higher rates of suicide and homicide associated with divorce. Some of these are temporary conditions, and the authors recommend programs for reducing the risk of difficulty due to divorce. They extend the hope that as society becomes more accepting of divorce, the risks for developing symptoms or experiencing discomfort will be reduced.

Goode (1974) noticed the similarities between widowhood and divorce.

"Unique qualities in each relationship make the universal experience of death *acutely* painful. No one can truly replace a person who has died but though each death and each divorce is unique, those who suffer them share many common experiences. They began with certain similarities in the life situation for both the bereaved and the divorced. These may be briefly listed: 1) the cessation of sexual satisfaction; 2) loss of friendship, love and security; 3) the loss of an adult role model for children to follow; 4) the increase in the domestic workload for the remaining spouse, especially in handling children; 5) an increase in economic problems, especially if the husband has died or left the home; 6) redistribution of household tasks and responsibilities."

Leslie (1974) compares Goode's (1961) analysis with that of Waller's (1967) research on the outcomes of divorce:

"Thus Goode's analysis supports Waller's in some points

and contradicts it at others. He did find that the majority of couples reach decision to divorce only reluctantly and over a long period of time; that for most of them, there is considerable trauma involved; that the minority experience some discrimination, and may be, sometimes, almost without friends; and that there is some economic deprivation."

On the other hand Goode found that most divorces kept their former friends and made other equally desirable friendships, and most quickly move back into dating and remarriage, and that their estimates of their financial situation changed positively.

When we look at the field of divorce, there have been numerous articles on divorce as a crisis. Holmes & Rahe present a life-hazard scale as quoted in Moos' book *Adaptation* (1976). A divorce represents a score of the 75 life-hazard units. Numerous changes that might be associated with divorce might take a divorced man or woman's score over 100, which would constitute not only a crisis but a significant stress that might render that person suicidal.

Briscoe & Smith did a recent study (1975) showing that there is a depression among divorced people that is similar to people who are hospitalized for depressive episodes and who have not gone through divorce. They also seemed to be somewhat similar to people grieving over the death of a spouse.

Heatherington (1976) has shown the negative effect of divorce upon divorced fathers (cf. particularly the loss of time with children because of depression since 90% of wives have custody). A study by Brandwein, Brown & Fox (1976) entitled, "Women & Children Last," describes the social situation of divorced mothers and their families. The study documents the damage and grief divorce heaps upon mothers who many times, particularly after age 30, are left as heads of households of single parent families.

Steinzor (1972) and Gardner (1969) had written books in terms of how to explain divorce to children. There are numerous other books on the subject by Krantzler (1974), Johnson (1977), and Maynes (1972) that have been written for people going through divorce to help them in their ability to cope, and to go through stages of grief and mourning, as well as starting a new life. This involves developing all sorts of new social ties to help them in readjustment. Finally, Singer (1975) has shown how divorce might be an opportunity to gain a sense of autonomy, and to provide new opportunities to get rid of early sexual restrictions and inhibitions that have caused problems, and to lead to a sense of individualization. Singer may be very perceptive in seeing divorce as an opportunity for new growth. But this readjustment to a new and perhaps a better adjusted state seems to follow a period of stress in which a person tries to reexamine the kinds of difficulties in their lives, and plans for the future.

DIVORCE ADJUSTMENT METHODS

Approach to divorce adjustment methods may include many different types of programs. Greteman (1979) has devised a program based on a series of lectures and exercises to foster an understanding of the current popular literature on divorce, and to deal with the feelings inherent in the divorce process. Gurman (1978) in his review of family and marital counseling suggests continued relationship counseling and/or family therapy to family members even after the separation or divorce. Fisher (1974) gives guidelines for divorce counseling. This is becoming more and more an important specialty in mental health services. Kessler (1978) has described various group approaches in building skills in divorce adjustment groups.

Weiss (1978) has devised a series of "seminars for separated" to present an educational approach to the personal problems due to divorce. Stewart (1976) has devised a program called "Beginning Experience." This is a kind of communication training weekend based on the Marriage Encounter model. Pino (1980) has devised Pre-marriage, Marriage and Re-marriage programs which build communication and behavioral change skills in a weekend group experience.

Programs for "Displaced Homemakers" resulting from divorce have been described in the book *Women in Transition* (1974). This is also the name of the group sponsoring a habilitation program which may involve the following elements: values clarification, assertiveness training, decision-making skills, managing finances, handling grief, legal aspects of divorce, educational and vocational opportunities.

Parents Without Partners and other support groups (e.g., Link) have been with us for over a generation. Such groups have provided not only support for the divorced adults but also give support to the family by doing group experiences involving the children as well. Such programs do preventive work inasmuch as they help ease the pain of divorce, and as Singer (1975) states, make divorce an opportunity for personal growth and to extend relationships. Thus, from pain comes personal learning and progress which may have never been recognized without the dissolution of a marriage. However, the complexities of divorce have just begun to be studied. The long term effects on children, policy implications of changing laws and cultural norms regarding divorce and the manifold implications of step-families and their extensions complicate the process of divorce. Future research will have to concentrate on the networks involving the divorced families and their surroundings; as well as the social, economic, and legal implications inherent in divorce and public divorce

CHAPTER FOOTNOTES

[1]Problems in data analysis necessitated a variation of this part of the research to be presented instead of the original methodology outline in Chapter II.

CHAPTER II

METHODOLOGY

OVERVIEW OF A THREE PHASE STUDY

The previous chapter was a broad overview of psycho-social aspects of the divorce research study. Uncovering the dynamics of divorce adjustment process was the aim of the present three phase research project. Phase One adapted the tool, psychological autopsy, to study (post-facto) what occurs in the course of divorce. Specific measures are presented to define important factors at each stage of the divorce process in a clinical sample. These same measure were given to unmarried, and married, individuals in the same clinical population to be able to make comparisons regarding divorce adjustment as opposed to other life stresses.

Phase Two utilizes the same divorce counselors population and measures as found in Phase One. The goal of Phase Two is to measure post-divorce adjustment by utilizing ratings of adjustment one year after divorce. A model for predicting divorce adjustment modified from Holmes & Rahe's (1976) Life Stress Theory, and Nye's (1977) Resource Theory was tested by Path analysis statistical method.

Phase Three of the study (Chapter VII) used a follow-up survey three years after divorce to compare remarried individuals from the divorce counseling group (studied in Phase One and Two) with remarried subjects who had attended divorce support groups. Aspects of remarriage preparation, marital adjustment, and the process of blending and reconstructing families were discussed based on the survey of the existing research literature.

The methodology for each phase will be discussed phase by phase. This chapter will provide a sketch of the test instruments and a fuller description will be given in the appendices.

PHASE ONE — MARITAL AUTOPSY RESEARCH

BACKGROUND OF MARITAL AUTOPSY

When people make a decision to separate or to initiate divorce, it becomes incumbent on them to try to understand what had happened in the marriage. Many separated or divorced individuals in turn seek therapy for this purpose. In divorce counseling one method of investigation which could be used is called Psychological Autopsy.

A. Weisman in 1968 provides a framework for this. This technique, Psychological Autopsy, was first used in Massachusetts at Cushing Hospital to try to determine the causes of death in an aging population. These were men and women who were the median age at death of 83. Of these people, age ranged from 68 to 100. The Psychological Autopsy technique has also been adapted to the whole field of suicidology, by Schneidman (1967).

Psychological Autopsy has been used to try to piece together why people have committed suicide, and to determine the cause of death. Sometimes it is undetermined whether or not a person has actually committed suicide. So a number of researchers might go back to collect personal documents, interview relatives and friends of the deceased and might include any kind of records one can procure on a client. Some of the pertinent aspects of the Psychological Autopsy includes the formation of the background information sheet. On this sheet one may have some idea of marital status, family background, sex, siblings, religion, occupation, past hospitalization, diagnosis, ward assignment, any transfer of the patient, and the termination of the cause of death.

A very brief outline for Psychological Autopsy is presented by Weisman (1968). The four important parts of this process include:

1.   What is a final illness?

2.   What happens in the pre-terminal period (just before the person dies?)

3.   The hospital course.

4.   The pre-hospital situation.

We can apply this scheme to suicide as well. As a person commits suicide, how do they function in the pre-terminal phase? What stresses occur? What happens to them after the stress? How does the person adapt to the stress? Were there attempts for help? And how does the person cope prior to the stress?

SCHEME

If we classify divorce as a crisis, we can modify the Psychological Autopsy model to analyze the marriage and its demise. There are five steps in the marital autopsy concommittant with Psychological Autopsy: dissolution, pre-terminal, course of marriage, pre-marriage, post-marriage phases.

MARITAL AUTOPSY SURVEY

RATIONALE — In an effort to provide some options for research utilization of this tool, some selective measures were taken in a pilot sample. They represent clinical ratings made during the course of treatment and some easily administered checklists that could be incorporated in divorce counseling.

SAMPLE — Twenty-five males and twenty-five females who were seen in treatment during their separation and subsequent divorce period were involved. Five formerly divorced couples were included in the study. Also, twenty-five married males, twenty-five unmarried males, twenty-five married and twenty-five unmarried females were randomly selected from the total treatment population. The setting was an urban, large eastern group private practice during the last two years. This practice received a majority of referrals from local industry whose treatment was paid for by comprehensive medical insurance coverage. Hence, there was a good representation from lower socio-economic groups as well as middle income groups.

MEASURES — The following measures are given as illustrations of possible categories related to each aspect of the Marital Autopsy.

1. Dissolution Phase: Usually when we ask the person questions such as: "When did you feel estranged from your spouse? What was the point when you felt "emotionally divorced?", they usually point to a particular incident[1] which was a stress—the proverbial "last straw."

   Reasons for Separation: This was a nine-item client checklist taken at intake covering the following categories (Re: Primary Reasons for Separation): abuse, infidelity, emotional abuse, physical abuse, spouse's infidelity, alcoholism, drug abuse, financial problems, disagreement over money, in-law problems, fear of long term commitment and other reasons.

2. Pre-Terminal Phase: Follows after this decision has been made, "How do they bring about the dissolution of the marriage? Do they go, for example, to try to repair the marriage? Do they move in another direction when they begin to make plans?" One example would be a person who goes about some preparations for leaving by creating a special "slush fund." This is money set aside that the spouse doesn't know about. They have already secretly looked for apartments and are economically preparing for singlehood.

   Pattern of Coping Mechanisms Employed: Clinician's ratings[2] of the predominant pattern of coping mechanisms that were employed by the clients. (Modified from Spiegel, M., 1976).

   In addition to the object-cathected, narcissistic, and aggressive types, a fourth category (Compulsive) work was added to create a more comprehensive scheme.

3. Course of the Marriage: What was it like? What are the peaks and valleys of the marriage? What kinds of crisis occurred in the marriage? How did they relate to children throughout the marriage? What was the satisfaction of the marriage? How did they relate to parents and in-laws throughout the marriage? How did they handle money? What was their secular relationship like?

Family Adjustment Pattern: Clinicians applied this rating scheme that categorizes the family into a four-fold taxonomy employed by Jackson and Ledered (1969): stable/satisfied, unstable/satisfied, stable/unsatisfied and unstable/unsatisfied.

4. The fourth important aspect in the Pre-Marriage situation: What was the person's adjustment throughout childhood, adolescence and early adulthood like? What were their personalities like? All of these things would be taken into account in doing a Psychological Autopsy.

a) *Childhood Environment*: Clinicians applied this rating scheme as utilized by Vailliant (1978) (refer to Appendix A). A zero (low) and a twenty (high) rating scale indicating the favorableness of a client's family environment as a child.

b) *The number of years living independently*: The question was asked at the intake interview.

Preparation for marriage is based on many factors. One condition found to be important here is a period of independent living prior to the marriage which allows for maturation to take place.

Figure 1 indicates the hypothesized direction of influence among the five variables: childhood environment, life change, resources, post-divorce behavior, post-divorce adjustment. Prior research in this area is presented in the section in Chapter I on "The Outcomes of Divorce."

Figure 1

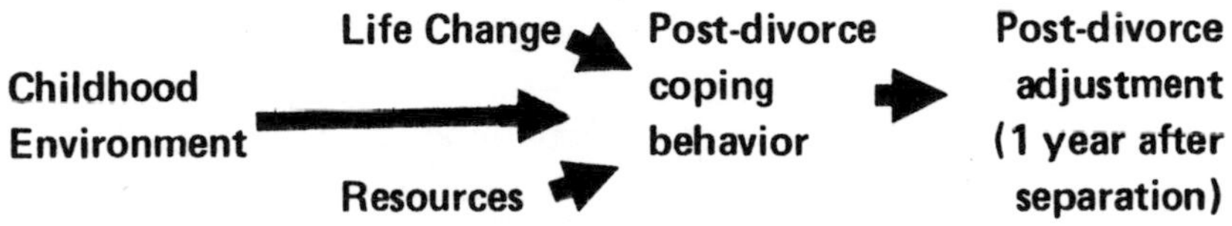

Life Change → Post-divorce
Childhood → coping → Post-divorce
Environment → behavior adjustment
Resources → (1 year after separation)

Figure 1 — Path diagram depicting relationship between childhood environment, life changes, resources, postdivorce coping behavior and post-divorce adjustment.

METHOD

Subjects: The divorced group in the previous study's population was utilized in this phase of the research. There were four sets of measures utilized in this phase of the research:

1. Life Change Units Scale — Holmes & Rahe (1976) (see Appendix A).

21

2.   Childhood Environment Scale — Vailliant (1978) previously described on page 20 — (See Appendix A).

3.   Resources Checklist — devised for this study (see Appendix A).

4.   Coping Behavior — Ego Functions Assessment — Sharp and Bellak (1978), two clinicians interviewed the patients and utilized this rating instrument. It is a valid, reliable and quantitative method. It contains ten sub-scales (see Appendix A).

5.   Post-Marriage: What coping mechanisms are employed? How does the person reconstruct a social life? What vocational, housing and visitation arrangements (if children are involved) are made?

a)   *Life Change Units*: (Holmes & Rahe, 1976) — an index of the disruption in life, patterns associated with the separation during the last six months. (See Appendix A)

b)   *Resources*: A client checklist of the types of resources they feel they possess following the separation (possible scores from zero to six); i.e., custody of the children, perceived adequate finances, an effective social support system (e.g., emotionally supportive family and friends), the use of positive avocational pursuits (enjoying their work, etc.) and whether the client has a lover (and reports positive feelings about their relationship).

22

PHASE II — DIVORCE ADJUSTMENT

The second phase of this research project tested a model for predicting post-divorce adjustment. The model follows Lewin's (cf. Bischof, 1975) suggestion that behavior was a function of characteristics of the person and the nature of his environment; i.e., B-F (P,E). Post-divorce adjustment would thus be seen as effective coping and that coping is a product of personality factors (vulnerability) and environmental factors - stress (i.e., life changes), and resources. Vailliant's (1978) notion of vulnerability is that it is based on a person's childhood environment; e.g. deprivation, traumas, family, conflicts, etc. Holmes and Rahe (1976) attribute life changes as a chief cause of stress which induces illness and emotional disorders. The importance of resources (e.g., environmental support, stable income, etc.) for individual and marital satisfaction has been reported by Nye (1977). It is proposed in the present research to be an important contribution to post-divorce adjustment.

PROCEDURE

Two clinicians interviewed and made ratings of the individuals on the Life Change, Childhood Environment and Ego Functions Scales at the beginning of therapy, and made ratings of the adjustment scale after post-therapy interview one year later. All subjects first filled out the Life Change Resources questionnaires.

ANALYSIS

A correlation matrix was computed separately for males and females. Then separate path analysis procedures (Kerlinger and Pethazur, 1973) were performed for men and women in the sample. This method allows for the inference of casual relations

23

among variables. According to Harren, et al:

"In the path analysis, the zero-order correlations between any two variables are decomposed into path coefficients. The path coefficients indicate the direct effect that a specific path has on a particular variable when all other paths to that variable have been statistically controlled. If the path coefficient between the two variables is as high as the correlation, then the correlation depicts a direct casual influence. If, on the other hand, the path coefficient is considerably less than the correlation, the effect of the one variable on the other is indirect. In other words, the correlation between the two variables to their common relationship to a third variable." (p. 394)[3]

PHASE III –
REMARRIAGE AND BLENDED FAMILY SURVEY[4]

The third phase of the research project surveyed the divorce counseling group three years after beginning treatment in an interview using a structured questionnaire. The questionnaire results of those who remarried were compared with remarried support group subjects who never sought professional counseling. This was done in an effort to ascertain the factors involved in the mental and family adjustment of both groups and to determine the contribution of both modalities to adjustment.

PROCEDURE

All subjects were interviewed individually by the same interviewer using the structured interview scheme, "Remarriage and Blended Family Questionnaire" (C. Pino), which follows.

Remarriage and Blended Family Questionnaire (C. Pino)
(Follow-up Questionnaire to Marital Autopsy Research)

Age_____   Age at Divorce_____
Number of Children and Ages_____   Age at Remarriage_____

1) What were the reasons for Divorce?
   a)   your reason?
   b)   Your ex-spouses reason?

2) Who left the marriage first?

3) What were the grounds for divorce according to the divorce decree?

4) What did you learn from the divorce?

5) How did the divorce affect you?

6) a)   What is the type of contact with your ex-spouse?
   b)   How frequent is your contact with your ex-spouse?

7) a)   Does your ex-spouse have custody or visitation rights?
   b)   If there are visitation rights, how often are they exercised?
   c)   Are visitation rights given or shared with your ex-spouse's family?
   d)   If so, how?

8) What is the extent of your responsibility for financial child-rearing, recreational, religious aspects of bringing up your children?
   a)   Of your ex-spouse?
   b)   Of you new mate?
   c)   Of significant others?

9)   What is the amount of your responsibility for your step-children with regard to question number 8?

10) What is the amount of contact of your relatives with your step-children?

11) How satisfied are you with your present marriage? (On a 5 point scale — 5 extremely satisfied to 1 extremely dissatisfied.)

12) What types of conflicts were present in the first marriage?

13) What types of conflicts are present in the second marriage?

14) How stable, do you feel, is your second marriage?

15) What needs are there for improvement in the second marriage?

16) What do you feel is different about being a blended family?
     a)   How does your spouse feel about it?

17) How has it changed you?
     a)   Your spouse?

18) What is the socio-economic level of your ex-spouse?
     a)   What is the socio-economic level of your present spouse?

19) What is the amount of support you receive from your relatives from past marriage? (5 extremely supportive to 1 extremely unsupportive)
     a)   What is the amount of support you receive from your relatives for this marriage?

20) How much power to make decisions do you feel you had in first marriage on a five point scale? (5 extremely powerful to 1 no power)
     a)   How much power do you feel you have in second marriage, on a five point scale?

21) What nationality, religious denomination, and age are you?
   a)   Your spouse?
   b)   Your ex-spouse?

22) How much freedom do you feel you have in the second marriage on a scale of 5 points?
   a)   How much freedom do you feel you had in the first marriage on a 5 point scale? (5 extreme freedom to 1 no freedom)
   b)   How much freedom do you feel you have in the second marriage on a 5 point scale? (5 extreme freedom to 1 no freedom)

23) How much affection did you have in the first marriage on a 5 point scale? (5 extreme affection to 1 no affection)
   a)   How much affection do you have in the second marriage on a 5 point scale? (5 extreme affection to 1 no affection)

24) Did you seek counseling prior to and/or after divorce?

25) What was the basis for choosing first spouse?
   a)   What was the basis for choosing second spouse?

26) How did you prepare for your first marriage?
   a)   How did you prepare for your second marriage?

27) How did your children react to divorce? (On a 5 point scale)

28) How did your children react to remarriage? (On a 5 point scale)

29) How do your children relate to your step-children? (On a 5 point scale)

30) How do your children relate to their half-siblings? (On a 5 point scale)

31) What advice would you give to prospective remarrying individuals?

32) How did your background prepare you for marriage?

33) How did your background prepare you for nearing divorce?

34) What is the role of your in-laws in your life?
   a) What is the role of your ex-in-laws in your life?

35) What are your hopes for the future for your family?
   a) What are your fears for the future for your family?

POPULATION

For Phase Three of the research, eighteen (18) of the Divorced Counseled group has remarried in three years. The re-married support group (n-18) came from the same geographic area. They had the same range in terms of age and socioeconomic level. They have met monthly for group discussion over two years.

A third group of remarried subjects (n-18) who were nominated by colleagues participated in a control group. They had neither been counseled nor belonged to a Divorce Support Group.

ANALYSIS

Most of the questionnaire items were ranked on a five point rating scale, thus generating five types of reactions — very well adjusted, well, fair, poor and very poorly adjusted. These were used to categorize the sample based on their answers to the 35 questions on the Marriage and Blended Family Questionnaire. The four types of reactions were then examined to ascertain the effect of divorce counseling, support groups and control groups.

CHAPTER FOOTNOTES

[1]Sheehy, 1976, describes "marker" events as that which change the course of an individual's life, such an incident is observed as a "marker" event. Other "marker" events have been delineated and an example is noted in the case study presented in this book.

[2]Variables 2, 3 and 4 were examined by independent ratings of two clinicians. Inter-rater reliabilities were: .75(2); .70(3); and .80(4).

[3]The results of this phase of the research is in progress and not available for the present volume. An alternative method was substituted in Chapter V.

[4]Results are presented in Chapter VII.

CHAPTER III

THE MARITAL AUTOPSY – RESULTS OF RESEARCH

RESULTS

Table 1 summarizes data (t-tests of the differences between group means) on the divorced counseling sample compared to randomly selected non-divorced outpatients on a number of variables. In considering Chronological Age, married males were significantly older (p. $< .05$) than unmarried males. There was little difference in the mean age difference between married males and recently divorced males or between unmarried males and recently divorced males. Married males were significantly (p. $< .01$) older than unmarried females. Recently divorced females show significant differences (p. $< .01$) when compared to divorced women. There was little difference in age mean between married females and divorced females. The only significant sex differences in age was between unmarried females and all three of the male samples. This female group was younger than the male group.[1]

The second variable studied was length of the marriage. The significant differences were found either between married

TABLE 1

PSYCHIATRIC OUTPATIENT DATA SUMMARY[2]
t-values (the difference between group means)

CATEGORY	1	2	3	4	5	6	7
Chronological Age	2.5	6.25 ***	1.7	4.70 ***	1.4	1.3	.01
Length of Marriage					0	1.6	19
Childhood Environment	2.7 **	2.5 *	1.8	1.1	2.6	1.8	103
Number of Years Living Independently Before Marriage					3.6 ***	5.0 ***	5.2 ***
Life Change Units	2.8 **	1.91	20.8 ***	19.5 ***	17.6 ***	17.9 ***	2.24 *
Resources			3.3 **	4.1 **			2.10 *

*Significant at p. <.05
**Significant at p. <.01
***Significant at p. <.001

Category 1 - Married males versus Unmarried males
Category 2 - Married females versus Unmarried females
Category 3 - Unmarried males versus Recently Divorced males
Category 4 - Unmarried females versus Recently Divorced females
Category 5 - Married males versus Recently Divorced males
Category 6 - Married females versus Recently Divorced females
Category 7 - Recently Divorced males versus Recently Divorced females

and divorced men or married and divorced females. No significant sex differences were found on this variable either.

Divorced women's scores on the Life Change units measure were greater than those of married and unmarried women
(reaching beyond the p. < .001) level of significance. Other sex
differences did not reach significance on this scale.

On the sixth variable, the resources scale, unmarried males
scored higher than divorced males (p. < .01). Unmarried females
had higher resources than unmarried males. Sex differences
favoring unmarried females over married and unmarried males
reached significance at the p. < .01 level. Finally, divorced
females fared better than divorced men on this scale.

Tables 3, 4, and 5 summarize (see Appendix C) descriptive
data on three variables from the divorced clients. Similar profiles
were found in comparing divorced males and females regarding
primary reason for wanting a divorce. Spouse's infidelity pre-
dominated as the primary cause for both males and females.

Ratings of coping patterns of divorced persons showed
some important sex differences. Ranked first for both sexes was
the narcissistic pattern of coping following separation. Ranked
second for divorced females was aggression. Ranked second for
divorced males was a pattern of overworking. This method served
as a way of structuring time to cope with anxiety.

Family Adjustment Pattern ratings were adapted from
Jackson and Lederer (1969). Table 2 shows that sex differences
in the ratings were noted—the stable/satisfactory marital pattern
was the most typical for divorced males. Divorced females tended
equally toward either the unstable/unsatisfactory or stable/un-
satisfactory pattern.

DISCUSSION

The Marital Autopsy techniques can be seen as a research as well as the clinical tool. The effort given here was to collect data on variables that would analyze various stages of the demise of a marriage. It also compares that data with information gathered on unmarried and married outpatients drawn from the same sample.

One important note to bring out at the onset in comparing these six groups of clients (unmarried, married, and divorced males and females) is that the divorced groups were most likely to be the first admissions for outpatient treatment, while the majority of the married and unmarried groups were likely to have been seen previously and to have a slightly higher incidence of hospitalization. The majority of the divorced groups came into therapy by themselves just prior to any legal action and usually showed great ambivalence about decisions to separate which were already in the planning stages. When both spouses entered treatment (the majority of cases), it was likely that they had previously been involved in marital counseling though only for a short period; i.e., premature terminators.

The *pre-marriage* situation was investigated using the Childhood Environment Scale (Vailliant, 1978). Results of the outpatient samples paralleled Vailliant's non-clinical male sample in that married males were more likely than divorced and unmarried males to have a positive home environment. A similar relationship held for females as well. Vailliant's notion assumes that positive childhood environment prepares the males he studied for a good marital relationship. The same idea could be extended for females.

A second aspect of pre-marriage research used length of independent living prior to marriage. Highly significant differences favoring longer periods of independence were noted with

33

married, when compared to the divorced samples for both males and females. Sex differences showed males to have longer periods of independent life in comparison to females. This coincides with Goode's (1956) study which found early marriage to contribute to higher rates of divorce. Although years of independence prior to living corresponds to age of marriage, it is more flexible in allowing for the slightly increased educational levels in this sample as opposed to the predominantly blue-collar sample Goode used. Independence fosters both maturity and a readiness for commitment.

Family patterns judged by the Jackson and Lederer's typology (1963) were used as a global assessment of marital relationships through the *course* of marriage. The trend toward stable/unsatisfactory relationships among males seemed more apparent in individuals who tended to repress conflict and rate their marriages much higher than their wives. They were likely to be shocked when their wives asked for a separation and the opportunity to date other males. There was a balance between the number of divorcing women in the stable/unsatisfactory category and the unstable/unsatisfactory classifications on these ratings. The former groups were older (later 30's and older) and were analogous in personality in males in this group (i.e., tended to be repressed, dependent individuals and likely to have their mates separate from them). The latter group were younger (mid-thirties and twenties) and acknowledged early marital problems and previous separations and were more likely to be employed and hence more financially independent from their husbands.

The *dissolution* of the marriage was studied by the use of a questionnaire — "Primary Reason For Leaving." This was an over-simplication since there were often multiple causes. Never-the less, infidelity accounted for over one-third of the separations while for both males and females, other reasons usually were not checked as secondary sources. This was the "unforgiveable sin" for many couples. Other categories regarding reasons for divorce showed peaks on the infidelity of self (as opposed to spouse's infidelity) and continued verbal abuse. Other categories were comparatively low on the list of primary reasons for separation. These ranking are at odds with Goode's (1956) analysis of divorcing women which placed higher emphasis on non-support, authority and drinking problems as primary reasons for divorce.

In older couples, later thirties and above, the "betrayed spouse" was more likely to not separate until their children approached adulthood. This corresponds to Bohannan's (1974) theory of the natural history of the marriage. His theory tends to focus on developmental crisis in marriages. The leaving of children demarcates a natural closure to a marriage dedicated mainly to the function of child-rearing. These couples had been estranged for years and had looked forward to a relief from responsibility. Younger couples either did not have children or if they did, did not feel so obliged to stay together as in the case of the older couples.

The *pre-terminal period* was a time between making a decision to leave (dissolution) and the actual geographic separation. This can be seen as a period of preparation for singlehood as well as a time for consolidating a pattern of coping with the loss of a spouse. This appeared to be a period of fear and marked distress and was the time in which many of these clients had entered treatment. Therapists global ratings of clients modified from the Spiegel (1978) scheme were used to ascertain coping style during this period. The predominant pattern for both sexes was the narcissistic coping pattern. This response category parallel's Lindemann's (1943) classic description of "normal grief" after a loss (e.g., somatic symptoms, depression, sleep and appetite disturbances and preoccupation with self, etc.). The most frequent categories showed sex differences, although non-significant.[3] Females were more likely to take an aggressive stance, preparing attack on the husband through lawyers, mutual friends, relatives, etc. This passing of blame abdicates responsibilities for the demise of the marriage. Males were more likely to bury themselves in their work (e.g., "moonlight" for extra money or put in overtime, etc.). This mode of adjustment is similar to one type of reaction to retirement. Reichard (1964) calls this the "armored-type personality." In this life style, anxiety is managed by structuring as much time as possible for work.

The *post-marriage* situation was analyzed by two measures: Holmes and Rahe's Life Change Units (l.c.u.) and a resource scale devised for this study. On the former, many types of changes are required of the divorcing persons. The scale itself has this built in by reserving 73 Life Change Units for divorce. Divorced males scored significantly higher than all other groups. They scored in the eighth centile in the LCU norms of the standardization group scale (i.e., compared to the standardization groups of males in the United States Navy). Divorced females scored significantly higher than married and unmarried males and females. One major source of difference between males and divorced females was that divorced males usually encountered a change of residence which didn't occur to the majority of divorced females. High amounts of life change have been realted to psychosomatic and emotional disruption. These implications for Life Change are well outlined by Gunderson (1974), Holmes and Rahe (1976), and Tennant and Andrews (1978).

The last variable studied as important in the post-marriage period is a resource scale. This rating scheme was utilized in comparing unmarried to divorced outpatients. Results indicated that unmarried women had significantly more resources than any other group. This may account for their greater happiness and lower level of symptoms as put forth by Bernard (1974) and Gurin, Veroff and Feld (1960). Applications of resources theory (e.g., Nye, 1977) has shown the importance of resources to adjustment and personal satisfaction.

CHAPTER FOOTNOTES

[1]All three t-values were significant at the p. < .01 level.

[2]Table 2 of means, ranges and standard deviations is given in Appendix B.

[3]Chi-square analysis non-significant at p. < .05 level.

CHAPTER IV

DIVORCE COUNSELING

Divorce counseling has become a recognized specialty in the 1980's. The drastic increase in divorce rates over the last 25 years necessitated this. The specialized training of a therapist engaged in divorce counseling should probably reflect not only a background in individual and marital work but also some realization of some rudimentary understanding of divorce law and procedure as well as issues involved in custody and visitation.

There are several models for divorce counseling. Probably the most comprehensive scheme is presented by Sheila Kessler (1975). She sees divorce counseling as stages of divorce (seven-fold), with specific intervention appropriate for each stage. The first stage can be seen early in marriage. The beginning of the divorce is set in the seeds of disillusionment. This disillusionment is a time in which the person realizes that the person they have married is very much different than the person they had hoped for. This disillusionment can often be dealt with well through communication techniques such as the Minnesota Couple Communication Training Program. The second stage is one of erosion. This erosion in a marital relationship is characterized by unfair fighting. Techniques for fair fighting, devised by George Bach, are important in helping to change the quality of bargaining and compromise in a marriage. Third stage is one of detachment. At this point, "emotional divorce" has begun. The person can be said to be in limbo in that they are undecided about whether or not to seek a divorce, and the therapist finds himself doing "limbo" counseling. This engages the client in the tortuous self-searching involved in a decision as to whether or not to leave the marriage. The fourth stage is one of physical separation. Kessler believes that a good deal of assertiveness training becomes appropriate at this time. This is a time when people may not always be supportive and a person must be prepared to be independent and to avoid attempts by others to induce guilt in him. He also must perhaps be more encouraged around vocational development lines in order to increase financial support at a time when he will need to be independent financially as well as emotionally. Developing new social ties and seeking appropriate legal advice often also necessitates assertiveness. This stage is one of mourning over the loss of a loved one. Just as one would lose a spouse through death, the loss of divorce must also be dealt with by overcoming one's depression and feelings of loneliness. The catharsis is particularly important at this point in divorce counseling and techniques to help facilitate this are important ones for a divorce counselor to learn. Appropriate support and, at times, crisis counseling are incumbent at this stage of therapy. The six stages of the divorce process is one of going into a second adolescence. Those who marry young or prematurely often thrive on a succession of flings or at least thrive on the ecstasy of a renewed romance at this period of time. Counseling centering on developing new relationships and overcoming fears of potential rejection as well as realizing past mistakes becomes particularly useful here. The seventh stage represents exploration in new commitments and stability of family ties in the nuclear family, or in preparation for a blended or reconstituted family. Techniques for the divorce counselor particularly center around helping the divorced person prepare for future crises as well as helping to terminate the therapy process.

Other approaches to divorce counseling include a crisis-oriented approach as espoused by Wiseman (1975). She feels the divorce constitutes a crisis in a person's life and short-term goal-oriented therapy should be the focus of counseling. Furthermore, the mourning over the lost spouse is necessary in order to facilitate independence. Through support and catharsis, this is achieved as seen on the fifth stage of Kessler's model for divorce counseling. Johnson (1976) believes that the process of divorce adjustment necessitates the ability to live happily as a single person. He helps to explore the irrational beliefs that lead to emotional problems and self-defeating thinking. This treatment approach follows Ellis' Rational Emotive therapy. The result of this type of approach should be the client's ability to analyze his own belief system and to be able to give himself positive self-verbalization that will shortcut emotional problems and increase his own self-esteem. Helping to develop social ties, being able to make demands of others and learning to say no are all assertiveness skills that are also encouraged. Exploration of activities and opportunities to make intimate contacts are a part of the dating skills program that Johnson also implements in divorce counseling. Fisher (1974) feels that divorce counseling serves to both support the person in the divorce period as well as inform them regarding preparation for legal issues that are inherent in the divorce process. Divorce counselors, hence, must have fair knowledge of divorce law in their particular state in order to be optimally helpful with their client. Bach (1973) teaches clients conflict management skills both in marital counseling as well as divorce counseling. The ongoing conflict when children are involved necessitates negotiation and sometimes mediation work. Mediation counseling can be a valuable service in helping the divorce parties better cooperate as parents. Another aspect of Bach's work is the need for a divorce ritual which he calls an "unwedding." This "unwedding" allows a person to go through an

40

official ceremony to break up the wedding and hence to celebrate possibilities for new beginnings. In addition to these counseling approaches, there are many education programs previously described which also help to aid in divorce adjustment. There are times where these informal support groups and education groups become psychotherapy as people begin to discuss difficulties. Pino (1980) has advised techniques for marriage counseling which involve two particular types of skills. The first is a need for an understanding of what has occurred before in the marriage and is accomplished through a technique called "marital autopsy." This technique, as described previously, is an adaptation of psychological autopsy which helps to develop insight into why the first marriage failed. Once the dissolution of the marriage has occurred, this process seems to be an important one before significant committed relationships can really flourish. The second technique that helps in the divorce process, according to Pino (1980), involves the necessity to work through the feelings of the separation. The use of a visual-emotive technique, called "Divorce Eidetic," an experience modified after Ashan's work (1977), has been developed for this process. Kaplan (1980) presents an approach to family therapy with single parent families, including important extended family members, for use in divorce counseling. Kaplan (1980) has utilized Minuchin's structural family therapy approach to diagnose and do family therapy with these families. Such structural reorganizations follow a family system approach to evaluating and treating the family. In addition to working with the adults in the family, divorce counseling approaches should also consider the needs of the children involved. Gardner (1970) has written a book for children to help them understand the process of divorce. It is his later work for professionals (1979) that imparts the knowledge of various psychotherapy techniques adapted for individual therapy for the children of the divorced. This particular approach utilizes therapy games as a way of developing the therapeutic relationship and exploring the difficulties the child is experiencing in divorce. Such games include a story-telling approach to therapy which can

41

be utilized with games such as junior scrabble and bag-of-words (feeling words). The object is to have the child tell a story regarding his feelings on a particular issue. The therapist then shares a story having a therapeutic motif or moral to help provide further insights for the child. There are various groups for children and parents that are helpful. One such program is devised by Korman and Stuart (1980). The parents' group includes the following topics:

1. How do you tell the child?

2. How much do you tell?

3. When do you tell?

4. What to share about the ex-spouse?

5. Problems with custody and visitation.

6. Change in lifestyle and responsibility.

7. Financial issues.

8. Feelings of guilt, anger and depression.

The group for children includes the following issues:

1. Divided loyalties.

2. Being pawns between parents.

3. Being used as a messenger.

4. Feeling responsible and guilty for the divorce.

5. Problems with custody and visitation.

6. Adjusting to a new lifestyle.

7. Fantasies of parents reuniting.

8. Feelings different from peers.

9. Teasing by peers.

10. Feelings of depression, anger and rejection.

These groups are usually eight weeks long, each session about an hour and a half each. Children between the ages of six and thirteen are commonly involved in such groups.

A rather comprehensive program for families undergoing divorce is projected by Sheffner and Suarez (1975). They see just a post-divorce clinic that works very closely with the court regarding issues not specifically mentioned in the legal proceedings. The post-divorce clinic involves families referred from the courts to a staff composed of psychiatrist, psychologists and social workers. Besides screening, testing (including MMPI) and psychiatric evaluation, ongoing treatment and mediation between divorced spouses is included in a comprehensive plan for treatment. This seems to be ideal, having a group of mental health professionals with close ties to the legal process being highly accessible in a comprehensive approach.

Thus the combination of approaches can be seen as useful in the divorce counseling process. Services for children are also advisable. Those who seem in need of treatment can certainly be provided with education and support groups; the latter provided through programs such as Parents Without Partners, the LINK program, and many others which can help to ease the pain of divorce.

CASE ILLUSTRATION

This is a woman in her late thirties who comes for counseling herself. She has decided to get a divorce. Her husband wishes to come in too. He wishes to save the marriage. He's hurt because he has some reason to believe that she might be cheating on him. In actuality, the woman was quite guilty because she felt she was engaged in a kind of non-sexual but very intense affair with another man. She claimed she loved him and wanted to eventually get together with him but had no illusions about this second man. She felt that he had a number of difficulties on his own and it made her very confused. She was concerned about getting a separation because she felt her own marriage was dead and yet she didn't know how to get from a marriage state to a divorced state. She was particularly ambivalent about re-engaging in a second marriage in a very hasty fashion, particularly when knowing the background of the second man and some of his liabilities as well as his assets.

In the first session she mainly talked about her decision to leave. We went through some important background history and reviewed the course of the marriage.

On the next visit, the husband came and he was determined to seek a contract for marital counseling. This was already obviated because his wife wouldn't consent to this. He was obviously depressed, as was his wife, but he was not in the same kind of conflict that she was. He seemed to still love her and want her, yet he noted a lot of deficiencies in their marriage and basically blamed his wife for the difficulties they were having.

There was an attempt to see the two together and eventually both consented. When they came in it was pretty much a free-for-all with open fighting, a lot of blaming, poor communication and a lot of remembrance of past hurts. The precipitating incidents were very clear at this time. Basically, both had gone on a Caribbean vacation hoping to reunite the marriage because there had been a lot of problems in handling the kids and relating to one another. Particularly, Fred's busy work schedule was something that Liz couldn't stand. It left her with a great many resentments toward him.

On this particular honeymoon it became very apparent to Fred that Liz was interested in this other man who was also part of the group on this package tour. Frequently Fred would catch her talking with him, looking at him, and it became pretty apparent to him that there was something going on. He became enraged and started a major scene in public. Later on, there wasn't much left to the vacation and both had a miserable time. This ruined the vacation for which they had been saving for a good part of the year.

When they came back they were still working out a lot of what had happened there. They had broken off social relations with this other couple but they became estranged sexually, although to a certain degree this had happened little by little over a year prior to this stress.

Fred, nevertheless, was still interested in maintaining the marriage. He felt that in court he would lose the children and wouldn't have access to them except for maybe one day a week as visiting rights.

It became apparent that divorce was imminent; both had sought legal counsel to protect their rights and both became inaccessible to marriage counseling. Fred found a lot of solace in friends and wasn't particularly amenable to individual therapy at that point in time, although later on he did come in for treatment when the realities of living alone and loneliness began to set in.

The wife was interested in individual couseling for herself. As Liz came in for individual therapy, the overwhelming guilt about her love for this other man and her disillusionment about marriage was very evident and there was a good deal of depression. She was very tired throughout the day. She would get up in the morning dragging. She had a number of psychosomatic complaints including loss of appetite. All of these symptoms are fairly typical in the person who is quite depressed. Also, we can see that as she pulls away from the marriage demands, her husband leaves to set up his own apartment, friends leave, and neighbors relate to her differently. Her kids want to know why this is occurring and her husband is mute about it. He refuses to answers questions claiming that since it was his wife's decision to divorce, he would say, "Ask your mother about it." The mother would then feel this tremendous burden of not only ruining the marriage for herself but also putting the kids in a position that was untenable for them. Basically they loved their father and they didn't see the same fighting patterns that the parents seemed to carry on in private. The children realized that there were some hassles in the marriage but they did not see how serious they were.

A psychological autopsy was attempted. The stress that was involved here at this phase was very clear. Looking at her writings (she kept a personal diary), it became apparent that she was planning for a divorce and had begun to make some preparations. She also shared this with a friend whom she brought with her in therapy. Her friend claimed that she had noticed a lot of these problems earlier in the marriage and felt that it was very sad that it had to end this way but that it was inevitable.

We can collect information from other parties provided the

person is willing to go through this marital autopsy and make their personal records like diaries, notes, letters, etc. available, as well as other relatives and friends. For example, the children were also brought in and they also seemed to notice that after the vacation, which had occurred several months before this couple came in, the marriage had declined rapidly. There were arguments and the parents were much more likely to stay out later to do things individually, to have separate friends and different interests.

When looking at the pre-terminal period, all of these things seemed to occur. Separate lifestyle beginning with a kind of individuality; whereas before, there was a much greater sharing in doing things with the kids. For example, family outings, even meals, were different in the pre-terminal phase of the marriage. It was pretty easy for her to see divorce as preferable to continued life as it was for them in this pre-terminal period since the decision for divorce had been made covertly by her—and it certainly wasn't announced. The physical relationship was changed, which was certainly one of the things that changed the husband's mind about maintaining the marriage, and a number of other things also changed so that this pre-terminal period was an agonizing, painful thing for both parties.

Reviewing the course of the marriage: In the first couple of sessions, it was quite evident that this marriage started off on a bad foot. They were economically very poor in the early years of their marriage. She felt she had made many sacrifices to get him through college and help him set up his business. There was a good deal of resentment about doing so. Later on in therapy, she presented a more realistic picture of their marriage and showed there were good times as well as bad, but in the last few years, the good times were far overshadowed by negative experiences, particularly traditional fighting patterns that were very difficult to break.

47

When we look at the pre-marriage situation in this particular case, we find a woman who came from a very repressed background. Her parent's attitude about sexuality was one of total condemnation. This was the first man she had dated seriously. She felt that she was breaking many of her long cherished religious beliefs to be involved in pre-marital intercourse with this man. This is going back to the 1950's and early 60's where mores were perhaps a great deal more strict than today. She was fresh out of high school and she wanted to break away from the home. She hastily married a man she didn't know very well. She entered marriage feeling somewhat compromised but relieved since she had gotten out of a situation in her own family which she felt was stifling her development.

At that point in time, she had little work experience and felt that basically her place was in the home raising kids and being a housewife. She had longed for this situation in the past and had gone through a period of idealism in adolescence that quickly left her after the honeymoon period. Then she found that she was pregnant and young, with little economic resources and with a husband who worked overtime and was trying very hard to be a good provider. He was also going to college at night in order to get through for job promotion and advancement.

The early years of the marriage continued on this course. She felt progressively more neglected, more deprived and more resentful. In the middle years of their marriage, their economic situation improved and they enjoyed a lot of parties and vacations. But later on in their marriage this wasn't enough. Somehow, a kind of intimacy was lacking and it was very clear that her own personal growth was stifled.

In terms of her readjustment, becoming an individual meant detaching her identity from that of her husband. It meant creating new friends and friendship groups and new opportunities for dating. When confronted with this after a couple of months

48

past the divorce, which occurred approximately six months after the beginning of treatment, she still was reluctant to even be in a position to be dated. For instance, she still wore her rings; she seldom went to parties where she would meet men; she refused to go to the bar scene. All of this now seemed to be against her dream. But, by and large, when new opportunities were presented to her; different dating groups, single clubs; she eventually went along and showed new patterns of readjustment.

Part of the depression and maladjustment could be seen as caused by her disillusionment with this other man. When she actually had the opportunity to date this guy and be seen with him in public following the separation, she found out that the guy wasn't anything like she imagined. He turned out to be an alcoholic and he was tied into a family struggle which was just draining his strength and jeopardizing his vocation. She felt that her own family was held together in a very fragile kind of way and would be devastated by the inclusion of this guy. She didn't even bring this fellow into the house to introduce to her kids. It was kind of like a double blow. Not only did she lose a marriage and the economic and emotional security that comes from that, but also she was disillusioned because she felt some real love for this other man and he wasn't anything like she had supposed.

I think it is very important to build self esteem; to work through mourning by providing catharsis, as we've mentioned previously, to provide new opportunities to meet people; to stimulate new courage and new activities. It is also important to straighten out situations with old friends so that there is no longer the kind of stigmatization that comes from splitting up the marriage where friends really feel an honest challenge to be able to continue relationships with both spouses. Oftentimes, this creates a great deal of dissettlement as we see the person going through this stress of losing not only the previous supports but the potential supports. Here are friends who have always been friends with both of them and now they are gone because they feel threatened by this divorced person entering their household. What it meant for her was that she had to change the nature of her relationship to married friends. She couldn't do things as a couple anymore. She could only do things with the female part of those members. Also, she had to develop whole new friendships, go out and get a job, and in all these things, there were essential mastery tactics and strategies that she had to develop. This meant new skills in living in terms of becoming more assertive in developing new relationships. In terms of skills in social living, certain role playing tasks were performed. A lot of these can be seen in a book by Goldstein called *Community Living and Social Skills* (1971).

The many roles played; such as, rehearsal for job interviews, and situations in which she had to meet men and relate as a single woman, were all practiced. This led to a renewed self confidence and ability to cope during this readjustment period following the divorce.

CHAPTER V

DIVORCE ADJUSTMENT RESEARCH

"Divorce Imagery, Post-Divorce Coping Strategies,
and Assertiveness"[1]

Abstract

A review of the literature is presented which indicates divorce is a crisis. An imagery method (Ahsen, 1977) was modified to study perceptions of divorced subjects towards their divorce. Subjects from two chapters of Parents Without Partners were administered measures of post-divorce coping strategies (Coping with Separation Inventory - Revised; Pino, 1979), and a measure of assertiveness (Rathus Assertiveness Schedule; Rathus, 1973). Six hypothesis were tested relating imagery theme, length of time since divorce and assertiveness to test divorce coping. Results from four hypotheses indicated that:

1.   An increased length of time after the divorce is associated with more effective coping (for females

51

only).

2. Women who perceived the divorce as a relief had higher assertiveness scores (not men, however); and neither men nor women employed more adaptive coping when compared to other thematic groups.

3. Men and women who perceived their divorce with hostile imagery had higher assertiveness scores, but neither group used more adaptive coping mechanisms when compared to other divorced subjects.

4. Adjustive coping was positively associated with higher assertiveness.

Although the thematic analysis of divorce imagery did not differentiate between individuals who perceived themselves as coping well or not well during divorce, the analysis provided a way to test hypotheses which have some theoretical support. Divorce imagery and coping were found to be relatively unrelated to one another. However, both were related to a third important variable—assertiveness.

Implications for assertiveness training and guided imagery as important techniques in divorce counseling are presented through two brief case histories.

DIVORCE AS A CRISIS

In an overview of this field of divorce, there have been numerous articles on divorce as a crisis and source of depression. Holmes and Rahe present a life hazard scale as quoted in Moos (1976). A divorce represents a score of the 75 life hazard units.

Numerous changes that might be associated with divorce (i.e., moving, economic reversals, separation from children) inflate a divorce man or woman's score over 300 which would constitute not only a crisis but a significant stress that might make that person suicidal.

Briscoe and Smith's study (1975) showed that there exists depression among divorced people that is similar to those hospitalized for depressive episodes, and who have not gone through divorce. Divorced individuals seemed to be somewhat similar to people grieving over the death of a spouse. Other studies have shown that divorce is a crisis. For instance, Herman (1974) suggests that people go through stages of grief in divorce similar to Kubler Ross' stages of dying, which are: Denial, anger, bargaining, depression, and finally, acceptance.

Heatherington (1976) has shown the negative effect of divorce upon divorced fathers; e.g., depression related to separation from their children. Brandwein, Brown and Fox (1976) investigated the social situations of divorced mothers and their families. The study revealed the damage and grief divorce reaps upon mothers who frequently (particularly after age 30) are left as heads of households of single parent families.

Bloom, White and Asher (1978) have discussed divorce as a stressful life event. Divorced adults have higher admission rates in psychiatric facilities and higher incidence of motor vehicle accidents. They also have a higher incidence of alcoholism, suicide, homicide and disease mortality compared to single and married individuals. Kessler (1977) indicated that, in general, better adjustment to divorce occurs in time.

GUIDED IMAGERY AND GRIEF

Numerous authors (Krantzler, 1973; Herman, 1974; Kessler, 1978) have suggested that divorce adjustment necessitates grieving in order to accommodate to the loss of a loved one. Morrison (1977) illustrated the use of guided imagery as a therapeutic technique instrumental in fostering successful grieving in bereaved patients. Guided imagery has been used effectively as a treatment strategy with depressed clients in the therapeutic systems of Ahsen (1977), Peris (1951), and Schorr (1976). The present author describes later in this paper the utilization of guided imagery technique with depressed divorce clients.

COPING WITH DIVORCE AND SEPARATION

Spiegel (1971) discussed three coping strategies used by bereaved individuals. They are the object-cathexis pattern, the aggressive pattern, and the narcissistic pattern. Lindemann (1944) in his classic study of grief reactions differentiates between normal and pathological grief reactions. In contrast to the normal grief, morbid grief reactions show the following tendencies: Delayed reaction, distorted reaction, increased psychosomatic symptoms, and agitated depression. McCubbin, et al (1971) discussed reactions of wives to prolonged separation due to their husbands missing in action status during the Vietnam conflict. They devised an instrument, the "coping with separation inventory," which isolates six distinct coping styles in separation. They were:

1.   Seeking resolutions and expressing feelings.

2.   Maintaining family integrity.

3.   Establishing autonomy and maintaining family ties.

4.   Reducing anxiety.

5.   Establishing independence through self development.

6.   Maintaining the past and dependence on religion.

Patterns number 4 and 6 were seen as maladjusted reactions to separation. Kessler (1977) found that the process of the decline of a marriage and subsequent divorce adjustment involves seven stages, each with its own pattern of coping. The stages she developed were:

1.   Disillusionment in marriage.

2.   Erosion of the marriage due to unresolvable conflicts.

3.   Detachment.

4.   Physical separation.

5.   Mourning.

6.   Second adolescence.

7.   Exploration and growth.

She has developed counseling strategies for each stage in this process.

ASSERTIVENESS TRAINING WITH DEPRESSED CLIENTS

Seligman (1974) describes depression as learned helplessness. He suggested that assertiveness training would be a treatment of choice for depressed clients. Studies done by Lazarus (1968), Rathus (1975), and Hersen (1976) have borne this out. Kessler (1978) utilizes assertiveness training as part of group therapy with divorced clients. This assertiveness approach has been useful in dealing with depression and in particular with the pain of divorce.

The above review relates adaptive post-divorce coping strategies to longer lengths of time after divorce as discussed by Kessler (1977), and to assertiveness (Seligman, 1974). Coping is seen as related to positive divorce imagery (e.g., divorce as relief or hostility); (e.g., R. Lazarus' (1966) cognitive appraisal model of stress would posit that events evaluated positively would be less stressful to individuals). The present study collected data on these variables and tested the following hypotheses:

1. The longer the subjects interval since the divorce, the more adaptive the coping strategies they will utilize.

2. Subjects exhibiting more positive themes (hypothesis number 2A Theme = relief, number 2B Theme = hostility)[2] in their divorce imagery will tend to employ more adaptive coping strategies.

3. Subjects exhibiting more positive themes (hypothesis number 3A Theme = relief, number 3B Theme = hostility) in their divorce imagery will tend toward displaying higher levels of assertiveness.

4. Subjects using more adaptive coping strategies will score higher on a measure of assertiveness.

METHOD

Subjects — One urban and one suburban chapter of Parents Without Partners (40 males and 40 females) in Western New York were chosen as the population studies. (Widowed subjects were excluded from the study.) Ages of the subjects ranged from twenty to fifty-five. They were tested in a group.

Procedure — Subjects were asked to project the image that most typified their divorce onto a blank 8½" x 11" sheet of paper. They were asked to answer on paper a standard set of questions regarding their imago as devised by Ahsen (1977, p. 147).

Following this, the subjects were given an inventory of coping strategies (the Coping with Separation Inventory - revised; Pino, 1979), and the Rathus Assertiveness Schedule (Rathus, 1973).

MEASURES

Divorce Imagery Thematic Analysis — A Thematic Apperception Test (TAT) type analysis of the responses of the divorce imagery questions was conducted by two clinicians. They determined for each subject the *predominant* theme of the imagery they produced. Inter-rater reliability was found to be .88 A table of random numbers was used to assign a subject to a thematic category when there was a discrepancy between ratings on an individual.

The themes that occurred were:

Rejection	(5 males, 2 females)
Loneliness	(6 males, 3 females)
Hostility	(3 males, 6 females)
Guilt	(2 males, 5 females)
Relief	(4 males, 4 females)

Rathus Assertiveness Schedule — Rathus devised this 30 item, self-report measure in 1973. It was validated on normal (Rathus, 1973), and psychiatric (Rathus, 1977) populations. Scores may range from -90 to +90, with an average score falling between 0 and +10. The split-half reliabilities on the measure are acceptable.

Coping with Separation Inventory - Revised — McCubbins' (1976) Coping with Separation Inventory was initially developed to analyze wives' reactions to husband's absence in a study on prisoners of wars. A factor analysis of the 46 item Q-sort inventory revealed six patterns as previously discussed. Pino (1979) revised the C.S.I. to make it amenable to divorced subjects.[3] The instructions ask subjects to rate each item on a 3-point scale — as:

How helpful was each coping behavior to you through the divorce?

(1) not helpful   (2) minimally helpful   (3) very helpful

McCubbin (1976), building on a stress model proposed by Lazarus (1966), suggested that coping patterns numbers 1, 2, 3, and 5 were adjustive methods of coping with crises, whereas patterns number 4 and 6 represent maladjustive strategies.

Statistics — A chi-square (Bruning & Kintz, 1968) was calculated to test hypothesis number 1. A two-way analysis of variance (Bruning & Kintz, 1968) was used to analyze the effects of assertiveness (RAS scores), and various divorce imagery themes, on coping strategies (CSI-R scores). Specific t-tests (Bruning & Kintz, 1968) were then used to test hypothesis numbers 2, 3 and 4.

Results — Table I presents means for males and females on coping scales (CSI-R), assertiveness (R.A.S.), and length of time since divorce.

TABLE I
Means for Coping (C.S.I.-R), Assertiveness (RAS), and
Length of time since Divorce[4]

| | CSI | | | | | | | Length of time |
	I	II	III	IV	V	VI	RAS	Since Divorce
Males	11.7	9.9	10.7	10.4	7.6	8.0	3.95	1.5 years
Females	11.4	10.7	10.5	9.0	7.9	8.8	-1.25	1.8 years

The first hypothesis tested the effect of length of time since divorce on coping strategies. Male subjects were categorized in a 2x2 chi-square table, as to length of time since the divorce (one year was seen as arbitrary boundary allowing for the usual mourning[5] which follows a divorce), and coping strategies employed, (if there was a greater proportion of positive coping categories; e.g., CSI-R subscales numbers I, II, III, and V, as compared to the maladjustive subscales numbers IV and VI). The same method was used to divide female subjects. A chi-square value of 1.5 (non-significant as p. < .05) was found on male subjects. On female subjects, however, a chi-square value of 5.0 was found (significant at p. < .05). Thus hypothesis number 1 — i.e., the longer the subjects interval since the divorce, the more adaptive the coping mechanisms employed — held for females, but not males.

Table II summarizes an analysis of variance on three measures — theme of divorce imagery, coping strategies (C.S.I.-R), and assertiveness (R.A.S.). The analysis of variance yielded the significant F-values (p. < .001):

(1) Subjects differed in scores for coping strategies employed, and

(2) Types of coping varied with the type of divorce imagery themes found.

This second value, the significant interaction of theme with coping, was more specifically analyzed by testing hypothesis number 2A; i.e., that a positive divorce imagery theme (Divorce as a "Relief") was associated with the utilization of more adaptive coping strategies. For males, a non-significant t-value (t=1.33, p. < .05) was found. For females, a non-siginificant t-value (t=.93, p. <.05) was found as well.

Thus, for both male and female divorced subjects, hypothesis number 2A was rejected. It may be noteworthy, however, that for males the t-value approached significance.

Another Divorce Imagery theme thought to be associated with adaptive coping was a hostile image of divorce. Hypothesis number 3A tested this. Significance was not reached for the male sample (t=-2.6, p. < .05) or for the female sample (t=1.6). In fact, just the opposite was found for the males; i.e., that hostile divorce theme group used less adaptive coping mechanisms than the other divorced males.

TABLE II
Summary of Analysis of Variance on Ratings

Source	SS	DF	MS	F	P
Total	8239	239	-	-	-
Between Subjects	1985	39	-	-	-
+/- Divorce Imagery Theme	6	1	6	<1	-
High/Low RAS	2	1	2	<1	-
Theme x RAS	41	1	41	<1	-
Error between	1936	36	53		
Within subjects	6254	203	-	-	-
Coping	569	3	189.0	9.49	.001
Coping x Theme	589	3	529	26.5	.001
Coping x RAS	31	3	10.3	0.52	-
Coping x Theme x RAS	84	3	49	2.46	-
Error Within	3895	191	19.9		

Hypothesis number 3A, that subjects exhibiting a more positive divorce imagery (divorce as a "Relief") theme, will tend toward higher levels of assertiveness was tested by a t-test of means. On the male subjects, a non-significant t-value was found ($t=1.98$). However, for females a highly significant t-value was found ($t=9.87$, p. $< .001$); thus confirming this hypothesis for divorced women.

Subjects with hostile divorce imagery (i.e., theme) were predicted to be more assertive. This hypothesis, number 3B, was confirmed at the .001 level of significance for males, ($t=14.9$), as well as for females ($t=11.2$).

On Hypothesis number 4 — subjects using more adaptive coping strategies will score higher on a measure of assertiveness (RAS) — significant t-values were found for both sexes (males: $t=3.3$, p. $< .01$, females: $t=2.15$, p. $< .05$). Hence, this hypothesis was accepted.

61

DISCUSSION

One factor hypothesized to aid in post-divorce coping was the length of time following divorce. The famous adage, "time heals all wounds" may not be necessarily true when related to divorce. At least its not true for males, although it was confirmed for the divorced women in this sample. This is consistent with results from Heatherington's (1976) study in Virginia. She claimed that men initially felt relieved two months after divorce. Later, however, (at one year) they felt that they had failed as husbands, and fathers, and were more likely to feel depressed than their female counterparts. Pino (1980) found significant differences between divorced men and women in the amount of time they had lived independently prior to marriage. He pointed this out as an important factor in post-divorce adjustment for women though unrelated for men since nearly all of the males in the study had lived independently prior to marriage. The sex difference found in this hypothesis may be due to this effect, inasmuch as women who had not had a previous experience living could initially have difficulties in coping but with time, adjust to this.

Those men and women who perceived their divorce as a relief (i.e., the Relief Divorce Image group), were not any more likely to employ adaptive coping than the other subjects in this sample (hypothesis number 2A was rejected). This was despite the fact that these divorced women were found to be more assertive than the other groups (i.e., hypothesis number 3A accepted, for women only). Quite the reverse was seen in men having a relieved image of divorce, inasmuch as they had lower assertiveness scores. Perhaps they felt powerless in their marriage, and hence, were relieved to be divorced, yet ineffectual in their coping.

The women who viewed divorce as a "relief" were more assertive, yet were not likely to employ more adaptive coping.

There was a difference of four years between the four males (average age 36), and four females (average age 40). Perhaps, this age of 40 constituted a midlife crisis (cf. Sheehy, 1975), which could decrease the divorcees coping ability despite their relatively higher levels of assertiveness.

Anger can be used constructively as a way to adjust to divorce as proposed by Bach (1974) in his approach to divorce counseling. This was the basis for hypothesis 2B and 3B. It was not borne out by the present research however. The hostile divorce imagery theme, males and females scored higher in assertiveness (i.e., accepting hypothesis number 3B), but neither the males nor females in this group used more adaptive coping mechanisms compared with the rest of the sample (i.e., rejecting hypothesis number 2B). In inspecting their responses to divorce imagery, a tendency was found among these subjects to generalize their hostility towards their spouse to other members of the opposite sex. This would undoubtedly decrease the likelihood of heterosexual contact, which Heatherington (1976) found to be associated with higher levels of self-esteem, and happiness concomitant with adaptive coping.

If assertiveness training is an effective treatment (Kessler, 1977; Lazarus, 1966; Hersen, 1976; Rathus, 1977) technique for depression common to the divorce process, it was predicted that those individuals who were more assertive would also tend to choose more effective coping strategies. As a general rule, high levels of assertiveness were associated with the utilization of more adaptive coping for males and females. Hence, hypothesis number 4 was confirmed.

Although the thematic analysis of divorce imagery did not differentiate between individuals who perceived themselves as coping well, or not well during divorce, it did test hypotheses which have some theoretical support, (as well as clinical support in the author's experience as a divorce counselor). These two

63

variables were found to be relatively unrelated to one another. However, both were related to a third important variable, assertiveness. A more definite breakdown (e.g., task analysis) of assertiveness skills useful in post-divorce coping should be undertaken as a follow-up to the present study. Such a study could unearth a more exact accounting of what constitutes efficient coping in such a crisis. This is a national crisis in that divorce affects at least 40% of American marriages according to Kessler (1978).

Implications for Divorce Counseling

Bach's (1974) notion of fight therapy for divorcee's proposes "creative exits." Although Bach was in that context helping individuals to break out of unwanted marriages, the technique could also be gainfully used in divorce counseling as a role play technique or as a guided imagery technique.

Another type of guided imagery technique can be seen in the case of Sandra. This 39 year old woman was seen in counseling prior to her separation, and consequently, through the first six months after separation. She was interested in another man after being detached from her husband (a "workaholic") for some time. Sandra felt a good deal of guilt about the divorce and was disillusioned in her relationship with this other man after discovery that he was a problem drinker. She became progressively more depressed and withdrawn and was obsessed by the guilt of leaving her marriage, and her fears of an independent life. She was instructed to produce divorce imagery, and asked a series of questions as recommended by Ahsen (1977, p. 147). The image she constructed was one of an angry husband blaming her for the divorce in front of her children who were in tears. She was extremely anxious, and crying when I then instituted progressive relaxation procedure which calmed her. Then, she was asked to visualize a time in her past when

she felt very self-confident and secure. Next, I had her re-exper-
ience the divorce image, superimposing the past image of
confidence and security. This combined Wolpe & Lazarus
(1966) "thought-stopping" technique (i.e., progressive relaxation and positive imagery) with Ahsen's (1977) superimposition
method of dealing with feared images. Other imagery techniques that could have been employed instead of this latter
one include emotional flooding (Olson, 1976), or implosive
therapy (Stampfl, 1967). Both are extinction procedures. Thus
she became less afraid by this formerly emotionally paralyzing
image and developed a new meaning for divorce. She was able
to reexamine the marriage, freed of the guilt that had chained
her through years of verbal abuse on the part of her husband.

CHAPTER FOOTNOTES

[1]Paper read at the Third Annual Conference of Fantasy
and Imaging Process, NYC, Nov., 1979.

[2]G. Bach (1974) would consider creative hostitility as a
positive way to cope with divorce.

[3]Ten items which dealt with the possibility of the husbands' return were deleted. Five other items were slightly
changed to make them appropriate to the divorced group. This
left six items per each of the six subscales of the test.

[4]When t-tests were conducted between means to test for
less difference on each variable, only one was significang (p. <
.05). This was on levels of assertiveness, males typically score
significantly higher on this scale (Rathus, 1973).

[5]cf. S. Kessler (1977).

CHAPTER VI

DATING AND COURTSHIP IN DIVORCE, REMARRIAGE AND THE BLENDED FAMILY

Dating and Courtship in Divorce

There are life cycles for individuals, for families and for divorces as well. Divorce is a process and some authors have a very detailed account of what is entailed in that process. Kessler (1975) suggests a seven stage theory of divorce which begins sometime after the honeymoon is over. The first stage is a disillusionment period where one or both spouses feel a sense of unfulfilled expectations. The second period is one of erosion, the wearing away of marital satisfaction. The third stage is detachment; the preparation for separation. The fourth is the physical separation itself. Fifth is a period of mourning that comes with the loss of detachment. The sixth is second adolescence and finally a seventh stage which involves personal exploration and hard work.

The dating and courtship period process has its season in the second adolescence in this divorce process according to Kessler, although dating can occur in almost any season. This dating period can be equated with adolescence in this particular period of time in the divorce process in that it seems to be a renewal of a search for a mate. There can be liberation that divorce will wield which will allow a person to date in a freer way than perhaps ever before. Sometimes without censure removed, there may be over-reaction where an individual may be dating several people simultaneously. This makes life even more complex but it may somehow create some sense of self-esteem which was lost in the hurt and rejection that may befall a divorced individual who has in fact gone through pain of a failing marriage.

Weiss (1975) talks about a similar process in divorce with the erosion of love followed by some continued erosion of love and co-existing with a persistent attachment the person retains as a result of this dependency on their spouse in the marital relationship. The loss of attachment can be a very slow and painful process and emotional reactions often include rapid shifts of moods. A necessary part in making the separation complete is building a new identity. This usually involves a re-examination of friendships and some amount of risk-taking to fulfill one's potential in one's life. At the same time, a divorced individual has to contend with pressures from kin, the possibility of increased financial responsibilities, and for the custodial parent, the increased stress of caring for children (many times with minimal assistance). In an attempt to start over, the advantages and disadvantages of dating are usually weighed in the divorced individual's mind. But under pressure of lonelinesss, some new strategies are taken and individuals who did not resort to dating bars, singles clubs and even computer dating may find themselves becoming more forward and assertive in this regard than ever before. Despite this sense of adventure, there simultaneously occurs a sense of distrust about others intentions. It's often quite natural for individuals in this stage to doubt not only the intentions of individuals they may date but sometimes even the information that the person they date gives them (e.g., regarding their marital status).

According to one estimate (Hunt 1966), at least 75% of separated individuals begin dating in the first year after a separation, with over 90% beginning before the end of the second year. Besides the possibility of a new attachment, other reasons include possibilities of companionship and the opportunity to make new friends. It can contribute to one's self-esteem, but there are also possibilities of rejection which impede opportunities to encourage dates. Intimately involved with the whole question of dating is the role of sexuality. The deprivation of sex after having easy accessibiliity in marriage creates more pressure for even casual sex. But there are many implications for sexual accessibility in the double standard that prior generations and, to a lesser extent even this generation, is still what many divorced individuals may believe in. More particularly women, who may feel some extent of guilt or at least being cheated by being sexually involved and not entering a more permanent relationship. To make things more complicated, the role of children presents a further obstacle to sexual activity. Divorced parents sometimes feel that this may damage the children if they are aware of their sexual activities.

Dating for Steven Johnson (1977) is a way of living the good life alone. This means going through "the emotional turmoil of separation" which could run the gamut of emotions: including anger, guilt, worthlessness and all the catastrophizing that a person may feel after the devastiation of feeling completely alone in the world. A necessity for a divorced individual, according to Johnson, is to be able to devise a job description for being a "fully autonomous" adult. This includes skills in daily living (cooking, housekeeping, transportation, money management, caring for children, pursuing a career, satisfying hobbies and interests, etc.), social attributes for friendship, and for dating and sexual relationships. Under the last category, the skills involved would be:

68

"initiating conversation with the opposite sex, finding ways of meeting the opposite sex, ability in attracting members of the opposite sex, ease in asking for dates, ease in refusing dates, dating regularly or often, a knowledge of and a comfort with dating etiquette and ease in communicating with the other sex in early contacts of dating, general ease in dating, ease in being affectionate, ease in reciprocating affection, ease in rejecting of affection, ease in making sexual advances, ease in receiving and reciprocating sexual advances, ease in rejecting sexual advances, general sexual ability, ease in sexual interaction, ability to communicate about affection and sexual behavior, ability to communicate in love-sex relationships, quality of love-sex relatioships." (pp. 124-125)

The implication is that one should be aware of one's functioning in all of these areas and could keep a report card on one's self. A divorced individual could also make goals for oneself and could even give oneself graded assignments so that progress could be made in the form of an action plan towards being able to be more fully functioning. Ideas that might aid in this process is finding a model to emulate, recognizing one's resistance to change, and behavioral rehearsal for challenging events, (cf., instance accepting or rejecting a date, etc.). One could chart oneself from day to day and reward oneself for good risk-taking behavior, for example.

Johnson presupposes that there may be a tendency to jump into a second relationship blindly because one cannot tolerate the loneliness. In order to do that, he gives guidelines on "loneliness tolerance training." This may mean gradually increasing your time alone from one time period to the next until you can experience full evenings alone without accompanying feelings of distress. It also places emphasis on the building of friendships and the importance of self-disclosing as another way to enjoy the single life. Practical questions in social life of divorced people involve: how to find people to date. This, Johnson feels, is a product of creating fulfilling social networks, involving people and activities that share interests. Also being involved in the world by being prepared to approach others and being accessible to being approached by them is important. He suggests, for example, "brainstorming" a list of interests that are comfortable for you and rating the density of other sex companions that may be involved in that particular activity. Therefore, a person could optimize their chances for finding people by selecting activities in which there would be a high density of people that they would want to potentially date. He even suggested ways to have casual conversations, of being positive by putting compliments in questions to other people and most importantly, to shortcut the "self-defeating sentences" that a person thinks of which may stop him from interacting intimately with others. This involves a good deal of practice and is not easily accomplished for many people. Therefore, he would suggest assigning yourself graded sequential tasks and rewarding yourself for accomplishment in your daily interactions with the opposite sex. It means practicing asking for dates and rehearsing rather possible rejection so that one becomes more and more resiliant to the possible destructive aspect of rejection.

As relationships are built, difficulties may arise with the different level of commitment that the individuals may have in the relationship. Each individual has his or her own sense of commitment timing. Some of this is due to chronological age. Other factors involved in this timing may be related to the ability to grow after a relationship that fails. There are bound to be mutual disappointments, sometimes individuals in their courtship period may even tire of one another. Involved in any close relationship is the necessity for good communication. This particularly means that one has to send messages to your partner that shows your personal feelings about specific behavior. Also important is the ability to actively listen to the other person. This means being able to paraphrase what the other person is saying. A third skill in close relationships involve negotiation. This may have been what was missing in the marriage and contributed to its failure. The fourth skill is obviously, self disclosure which is to be able to share with another person. All of these form the basis for a secure relationship and over the process of time may eventuate in a marriage or a marriage-like relationship. However, even if it doesn't occur, Johnson feels that these are the earmarks of a mature individual who is fully autonomous and can have an extremely fulfilling life as a single person.

Krantzler (1973) finds that divorce forces new kinds of behavior. This means first a necessity to mourn the relationship and to live through that time to finally be able to channel oneself away from fits of weeping and self-pity. It means being able to channel your energies towards constructive building of relationships and reconstituting a stable family and finally discovering one's own strengths and realizing one's assets. Fisher (1975) suggests some rules regarding the etiquette of divorce and she feels that there are new proprieties and their graceful way to handle situations that arise when marriage breaks up. This involves what to tell other people about the separation which also has implications for noting one's availability. She also suggests ways to handle gossip, introducing dates to your children, ways to handle relationships with men who have children and discriminating between things that should be told to a date versus things that should not be told. One important note, according to Fisher, is that one should stop long enough to reflect at the types of people that you are dating since they generally may reflect your own stage of personal growth.

Remarriage

According to Leslie (1975) persons who have been married before have higher probabilities of remarrying than of single persons of getting married for the first time. For example, in the age period 20-24, the probability that a divorced woman will remarry is twice that of a single woman marrying. At older ages, differences gradually increase in favor of previously divorced women. Divorcees are also more likely to remarry at this age than in the 25-30 range than widows. For divorced men, the probability of remarrying is greater than widowed men and also single men age by age. When divorced males are compared to females, divorced males have higher probabilities at each age level than their female counterparts of those in their early 30's. More than one divorced man out of three will remarry compared to one out of five divorced women. Racially, there is higher remarriage rates for blacks than for whites, as indeed there are higher divorce rates for blacks than for whites.

Actually remarriage covers a number of different types of marriage when we look at the possibility of a divorced man or woman marrying single widowed or a divorced man or woman. Table 1 provides the distribution of remarriage by previous marital status into populations.

Overall, more than 75% of men remarry and over 70% of women remarry. "Jacobson reports that one third of women who remarry after divorce do so within five years." Leslie (1975, page 729).

In 1977 the mean age of remarriage of previously divorced brides was around 30.2 years compared to the mean age of remarriage of previously divorced grooms being at 33.6 years. Over the 70's, there has been a decline in the mean age of remarriage (*Marriage & Divorce Today*, August 20, 1979). Leslie (1975) suggests that courtship and weddings are different in remarriage than in marriage, with women remarrying being less likely to have a formal engagement, to receive an engagement ring and a trend towards shorter engagement periods. They also tended to have a lower percentage of church weddings. According to Garuk (1980), college educated women take one year

Table 1
**The Distribution of Remarriages by Previous Marital Status
in Two Populations**

Previous Marital Status	1947 Cases in Utopolis*	13,088 Cases in Seattle
Divorced man-single woman	10.7% (403)	18.2% (2397)
Divorced man-widowed woman	4.5% (87)	5.4% (721)
Divorced man-divorced woman	16.4% (319)	23.3% (3057)
Single man-divorced woman	21.5% (419)	29.8% (3917)
Single man-widowed woman	9.0% (176)	8.0% (1046)
Widowed man-single woman	12.9% (251)	3.4% (459)
Widowed man-widowed woman	9.3% (182)	6.8% (797)
Widowed man-divorced woman	5.6% (110)	5.2% (694)

*Utopolis is a hypothetical community constructed around 2009 remarriages which are assumed to be the total remarried population of the community. Previous marital status was unknown in 62 of the 2009 cases studied.

Source: Jessie Bernard, *Remarriage: A Study of Marriage*, New York: Dryden Press, 1956, p. 9; and Charles E. Bowerman, "Assortative Mating by Previous Marital Status, Seattle, 1939-1946," *American Sociological Review* 18 (April 1953), p. 171.

longer to remarry and have a lower remarriage rate. Studies done by Locke (1951), by Burgess & Cottrell (1939), by Terman (1938) suggests that remarriages reported to be either very happy or happy are actually quite high-about three quarters of those remarried persons surveyed in Leslie (1975). Despite this, however, the divorce rate for remarried individuals is 44% compared to 40% of first marriages. These studies have been closely replicated by Glenn & Weaver (1977) finding a high percentage of satisfaction in remarried individuals very comparable to never divorced males and females. Bernard (1956) suggests that as a result of going through a divorce once, one is less afraid of re-experiencing and has "learned the ropes," so to speak, of legally and emotionally surviving a divorce.

Garfield (1979) notes two particular trends in examining divorced people who remarry: 1) They tend to choose other divorced people more often than not, (see Table 1[1]); 2) They gravitate toward partners whom they may perceive to be completely different in character from the first spouse, (c.f., Hunt, Hunt & Westoff, 1977). "More specifically, this latter reference relates to the fact that divorced individuals sought out those who display for them the traits of warmth, maturity and capacity for commitment as opposed to attractiveness and wealth which had characterized their earlier choices," (Garfield, 1975, page 5). These individuals were also more likely to choose partners whose interests reflected their own and who had concomitant values and needs. Their conclusions are similar to those of Jessie Bernard (1956) who felt that the first marriage was seen by remarrying individuals as an "apprenticeship" in order to increase their capacity for maturity and commitment in their second marriage. Another trend is a tendency towards a trial marriage among the remarried. Hunt (1956) reported that over a third of the two person (male-female) unmarried households in America are occupied by at least one formerly married person. While these pre-remarital relationships tend to be erratic in intensity, however, the mood shifts in this relationship may be due to the fear of becoming emotionally vulnerable again. The rationale for remarriage relates to needs for companionship, many emotional needs and sex. Both Bernard (1973) and Glenn & Weaver (1977) have suggested when remarriage occurs, a remarried man's satisfaction tends to be higher than the remarried woman's satisfaction physically, socially and psychologically. Bernard (1956) suggests that role changes and societal changes upgrading the status of women and sharing of roles are necessary functions in order to increase the woman's marital satisfaction.

Adjustment in remarriage involves several different aspects. In the area of sexual adjustment, Leslie (1975) finds that the sexual participation and sexual satisfaction in a second marriage is likely to be greater than in the first marriage. Not only will they profit from greater sexual knowledge than in the first marriage but the probability of premarital intercourse between the mates is more likely to occur in a second marriage than in the first marriage. In the area of social life, a new couple may find some difficulties in relating to old friends. They may necessitate giving up some old friendships and allowing for new ones. The new relationship will more likely occur with people who are not acquainted with the former marriage. Thus the remarrying couple is off to a fresh start in the social arena. Adjustment to former partners also plays an important role in the remarriage. One likely difficulty even if the person has worked through the difficulties in the prior relationship is that the former spouse may be likely to intrude on the new relationship when there are children involved. Finally, when stepchildren enter the scene, there usually is an ongoing process of becoming a new family which serves as a challenge and sometimes may interfere with and create difficulties for the stepparent. In summary, there are "three factors working to make a second marriage successful: the learning which occurred during the first marriage, changes in motivation which follow an unsuccessful marriage, and changes associated with increasing age and maturity" (Leslie, 1975, page 753).

Stepfamilies and Blended Families

In today's rapidly changing world where divorce and remarriage have shown an increasing trend over the last generation, the idea of blended families seems to be becoming a normal part of our society. Bernard (1956) in a large scale study of over 2000 remarriages found that 60% of both men and women who remarried following divorce had children from a first marriage.

Toffler (1978) suggests that over 30% of American children at some point or another in their lives live in a blended family. Vischer & Vischer (1979) provide a much lower (conservative) estimate of 13% of families in which one of the adults is not a biological parent with living arrangements being provided for children under 18. This low figure may be due to the fact that step-relationships exist but those children did not necessarily reside in the families studied. Not all of the stepparents, however, are the result of a divorce. Other ways of acquiring a stepparent may be through the death of a parent, or being born out-of-wedlock. I will confine my remarks to those children who are involved in remarriage. The effects of divorce on children have been well documented in studies done by Heatherington (1978), by Wallerstein & Kelly (1980), by Kulka & Weingarten (1979), among others. While the results have been equivocal the general consensus is that the most adjustment problems are seen in the first year. Heatherington (1978) "Five years after the breakup, 34% of the kids are happy and thriving. 29% are doing reasonably well but 37% are depressed in an in-depth study of 60 families, traces patterns of different outcomes as in married family what counts the most are the two parents "(positive) attitudes," (Wallerstein & Kelly, 1980, page 67).

Particularly important is the ability of the former spouses to continue to cooperate in the care of their children. Kulka & Weingarten (1979) show in their long term study of children of divorced as grownups tend to indicate that they differ little in overall adjustment from children reared in intact homes. However, they seem less happy and complain more about psychosomatic symptoms. The effects of remarriage upon children has been the subject of numerous studies. Nye (1957) found that the adjustment of children was better in remarried homes than in unhappy, unbroken homes. Bowerman & Irish (1962) in a large scale national sample with junior and senior high students found that the adjustment of children towards stepparents was poorer than toward the real parent of the same sex. Generally adjustment to stepfathers was better than to stepmothers. Burchinal (1964) found few differences on personality measures of grade point average between children from unbroken homes, of broken homes and remarried homes except for the fact that children from unbroken homes tended to be absent the least number of days from school. Goode (1956) indicated that remarriage tended to regularize the position of children following the trauma of divorce and that the conflicts between children and new parents decreased with time.

In Duberman's research (1973) the large majority of parent-stepchildren relationships (64%) were rated excellent on a parent-child relationship questionnaire. Bernard (1956) concludes that most remarriages are not harmful to children and that children's adjustment to remarriage is a product of three factors: "1) the attitudes of the children to the remarriage; 2) new parent as a salvaging force; and 3) the inherent resiliency of human nature" (in Leslie, 1975, page 742). This would tend to militate against the idea of "the wicked stepmother or the aloof stepfather" as seen in the folk caricatures of stepparents. Duberman focuses on step-sibling relationships. The quality of these relationships, she feels, is as good as the adjustment level of the remarriage. Another important factor in the adjustment of stepchildren is the question of an absent biological parent. She noted that this seemed to have a detrimental effect on the stepparent-stepchild relationship.

Some of the negative aspects involved in remarriage can be seen in some of the research literature. Bowerman & Irish (1962), for instance, found that in all aspects homes involving step-relationships proved more likely to have stress, ambivalence, and low cohesiveness than normally intact homes did. Fast & Cain (1966) found that difficulties were seen in role functioning in stepparent homes and it is stress of being a step-parent. McCormack (1974) in reviewing the literature yields conclusions similar to Bowerman & Irish (1962), and suggests that there be a straightforward recognition that the stepparent is not the parent, thus allowing the child emotional room to feel loyalty to his biological parent and think well of himself at the same time. Virginia Satir (1972) identifies issues for blended families which include: 1) a necessity of making psychological room for previously existing families; 2) the importance of working through pain from the divorce; 3) the importance of regular conferences on the part of the ex spouses regarding the children, 4) decrease expectation in the second marriage for assuming high expectations for the marriage and stepparenting (without realizing the possible antipathy shown on the part of the stepchildren towards their stepparents).

Vischer & Vischer (1978) suggests four common myths that impede family functioning: 1) the myth of instant love; 2) the myth of the death of a spouse makes stepparenting easier; 3) the myth that stepfamilies are the same as nuclear families; and 4) that stepchildren are easier when living in the home. They suggest that the poorly defined role of the stepparent, particularly the stepfather, is identified as an issue that creates conflicts particularly in the financial and disciplining roles. Vischer & Vischer (1979) suggest the following guidelines for stepfamilies: 1) they suggest the importance to arrange time alone or allow room for the parents own relationship to grow in the remarriage; 2) forming new relationships in the stepfamily through activities involving different subgroups can be important, (e.g., stepfather and stepchildren might collectively work on a project together); 3) preserving the loyalties towards the original parents are important; 4) allowing time for the relationship to emerge between stepparents and stepchildren. This may demythologize the idea of instant love; 5) the realization that stepfamilies are different structurally and emotionally from first families can be helpful in being able to tolerate upsetting behaviors on the part of stepchildren that result from feelings of insecurity and loss; 6) open relationships between ex spouses are a necessity in order to avoid difficulties; 7) family negotiation sessions may be helpful for the stepfamily to communicate difficulties as they arise; 8) since being a stepparent is a difficult role, it's important that parents devise a role for themselves that is different and does not compete with natural parents; 9) visiting stepchildren may find the neighborhood strange so that it would be imporant if they would be included in stepfamily projects and chores. It might be helpful if they brought a friend with them for the visit. Also, non-custodial parents and stepparents must make clear their expectations to the visiting children, 10) it may be important for the couple to minimize to some extent the sexual aspects of the household, although children should still receive affection and be aware of the tenderness between the couple.

Educational Programs for Remarried and Stepfamilies

Walker, et al., (1979) review literature on educational and treatment applications to remarriage. Many of the articles she quoted dealt with utilization of family therapy and child gui-dance to help in the process of blending or reconstituting families. Programs of an educational nature may focus on remarriage. One model is given by Nichols (1979) in his "Problems in a Second Marriage" series. This series areas of concern in remarriage include: "(a) reactions to and residues from the first marriage and its ending on the part of both spouses in the second marriage, (b) children, and (c) finances, possessions and inheritance matters," (page 157). Pino (1980) has devised a program for personalizing premarriage and remarriage in a workshop format. This includes communication and conflict management training, marriage contracting. In reviewing personal history and conflicts with stepchildren in an effort to work toward higher effective family functioning the marriage.

Jacobson (1979) has developed a program for stepparents. This involves the difficulties in childrearing of stepchildren, feelings of being rejected by stepchildren, problems with the ex spouse over care of children. Messenger (1979) has developed a curriculum for preparation for remarriage course.

> "The proposed content includes: 1) feelings related to the first marriage and divorce. . .; 2) remarriage adjustment . . .; 3) division of labor in the present marital household . . .; 4) perception of role relationships. . .; 5) responsibility of the new partner. . .; 6) exchange of views between present couple on child rearing. . .; 7) perceptions of what constitutes a 'happy family life'. . .; 8) feelings about financial arrangements. . .; 9) feelings about continued relationships between ex spouse and/or ex spouses kin, between children and absent parent and kin. . .; 10) feelings about partners children living with ex spouses visiting regularly in the present household." (page 198)

Finally the role of divorce support groups and remarried support groups can play a very important role in the maintenance of post-divorce successful adjustment. The experience of Parents Without Partners and programs for divorced Catholics (e.g., Link) have played an important role in American society today. They provide important self help as well as noted in similar groups by Huvitz (in Roman & Trice, 1974).

In conclusion, post-divorce dating and courtship involves a realization of many skills. It comes as a natural phase of the divorce life cycle, and it involves some amount of risk taking. Remarriage is on the rise and seems to involve a more rational process of mate selection, and has higher levels of satisfaction than the first marriage, similar to intact homes. However, there are certain risks in remarriage thus the stability rates are not quite as high as in first marriages. Blended families propose a new challenge and education programs and support groups can be extremely helpful in paving the way for effective family functioning in reconstituted families.

CHAPTER FOOTNOTES

[1]New figures (c.f., Glick, 1978) favor divorced man-divorced woman as the most popular combination in contrast to Table 1.

CHAPTER VII

REMARRIAGE AND BLENDED FAMILIES

A Comparative Study of a Self-Help Remarried's Support Group,
Treated and Untreated Remarried Subjects

This research was undertaken in order to study the process
of adjustment from divorce to remarriage and the forming of a
blended family, remarried therapy clients, members of (a divorce) remarried support group and an untreated remarried group
completed questionnaires. Categories of responses were grouped
accordingly to areas of divorce adjustment, remarriage adjustment and child rearing. These categories tested hypotheses about
the greater difficulty in adjustment for the priorities of the
treatment group compared with the other two groups. These
hypotheses were confirmed and questionnaire responses were
analyzed to describe differences in these three areas for each
group. Responses of support group members were similar to
those of untreated remarried subjects; to the groups indicating
higher remarital adjustment, and functioning as step-families.
The contributions of therapy and support groups are also discussed.

Blended Families

In today's rapidly changing world, where divorce and re-marriage have shown an increasing trend over the last genera-tion, the idea of blended families seems to be becoming a normal part of our society. Bernard (1956) in a large scale study over 2000 remarriages found that 60% of both men and women who remarried following divorce had children from a first marriage. Toffler (1978) suggests that over 30% of American children at some point or another in their lives live in a blended family.

Remarriage and reconstituting a family usually has positive effects on children according to several studies (e.g., Nye, 1957; Bowerman and Irish, 1962 Burchinel, 1964; Goode, 1956; Duberman, 1973, Bernard, 1956).

Some of the negative aspects involved in remarriage can be seen in some of the research literature. Bowerman & Irish (1962), for instance, found that in all aspects homes involving step-relationships proved more likely to have stress, ambivalence and low cohesiveness than normally intact homes did. Fast & Cain (1966) found that difficulties were seen in role functioning in stepparent homes and it is stress of being a stepparent. McCor-mack (1974) in reviewing the literature yields conclusions similar to Bowerman and Irish (1962) and suggests that there be a straightforward recognition that the stepparent is not the parent, thus allowing the child emotional room to feel loyal to his bio-logical parent and think well of himself at the same time. Virginia Satir (1972) identifies issues for blended families which include: 1) a necessity of making psychological room for previously exist-ing families; 2) the importance of working through pain from the divorce; 3) the importance of regular conferences on the part of the ex spouses regarding the children; 4) decrease expectation in the second marriage for assuming high expectations for the marriage and stepparenting (without realizing the possible antipathy shown on the part of the stepchildren towards their stepparents.) Vischer and Vischer (1979) present many helpful suggestions for step-families.

Educational and Treatment Programs for Remarried and Step-families

Walker, et al (1979) review literature on educational and treatment applications to remarriage. Many of the articles she quoted dealt with utilization of family therapy and child guidance to help in the process of blending or reconstituting families. Family therapy approaches the blended families are presented by Bitterman (1968); Goldman, (1977); and Goldstein, (1974). A model for group therapy for stepfathers and their wives has been devised by Mowatt (1972).

Programs of an educational nature may focus on remarriage. One model is given by Nichols (1979) in his "Problems in a Second Marriage" series. This series' areas of concern in remarriage include: 1) reactions to and residues from the first marriage and its ending on the part of both spouses in the second marriage; 2) children and 3) financial possessions and inheritance matters (page 157). Pino (1980) has devised a program for personalizing premarriage and remarriage in a workshop format. This includes communication and conflict management training, marriage contracting. In reviewing personal history and conflicts with stepchildren in an effort to work toward higher effective family functioning in the marriage.

Jacobson (1979) has developed a program for stepparents. This involves the difficulties in childrearing of stepchildren, feelings of being rejected by stepchildren, problems with the ex spouse over care of children. Messenger (1979) has developed a curriculum for preparation for remarriage course.

Finally the role of divorce support groups and remarried

support groups can play a very important role in the maintenance of post divorce successful adjustment. The experience of Parents Without Partners and programs for divorced Catholics (e.g., Link) have played an important role in American society today. They provide important self help as well as noted in similar groups by Huvitz (in Roman & Trice, 1974).

Raschke (1977) found that Parents Without Partners Support Groups play an important role in post-divorce adjustment. An evaluation of support groups for separated and divorced Catholics has been conducted by Foy and Kircher (1979). They found that "the need for social (52%) and emotional support (47%) were primary reasons given by those who attended the groups" (page 2). In many areas, as in Buffalo area (where the current research is taking place), these groups often retain membership after they have remarried. Thus, continued support is provided in the transition to blended families.

In conclusion, remarriage is on the rise and has higher levels of satisfaction than the first marriage, similar to intact homes. However, there are certain risks in remarriage, thus the stability rates are not quite as high as in first marriage (Leslie, 1975). Blended families propose a new challenge. Therefore, therapy, education programs and support groups can be extremely helpful in paving the way for effective family functioning in reconstituted families. The present research compared subjects who have been in therapy before and after remarriage with subjects in remarried support groups and untreated remarried individuals, to study the similarities and differences among groups.

Methodology for Remarriage and Blended Family Research

Rationale research project surveyed a group of remarried counseling subjects after beginning treatment in using a structured questionnaire. The questionnaire results of those who re-married were compared with remarried support group subjects who never sought professional counseling, and a third group of remarried subjects who had either been in therapy or a support group. This was done in an effort to ascertain the factors involved in the mental and family adjustment of both groups and to determine the contribution of both modalities to adjustment.

While the present research is primarily a descriptive study, prior research (Pino, 1980b) suggested some specific hypotheses for this study. It was assumed that the three groups represented very different populations. The treatment group being most poorly adjusted. Particularly, the treatment group was anticipated to have more difficulty in divorce adjustment and thus also have a deleterious effect on their children. Additionally, they would be more likely to be rejected by their first spouse.

Sample

Remarried therapy sample—six males and twelve females were seen in treatment during their separation and subsequent divorce and remarrying period, (usually a combination of individual, marital and family therapy for at least one year and more sporadically for as long as ten years). The setting was an urban, large eastern urban private practice. This practice received a majority of referrals from local industry whose treatment was paid for by comprehensive medical insurance coverage. Hence, there was a good representation from lower middle to upper middle socio-economic groups. All subjects were caucasion, half were Catholic denomination. The range of the clients were from 21 to 47 with a mean age of 35.2 years. Of the 18, twelve were diagnosed as neurotic, six as character or personality pattern disorders, and two as schizoid types.

Remarried Support Group

The remarried support group (N=8—6 males, 12 females) came from the same geographic area, and had the same range, in terms of age and socio-economic level. All were caucasian. They had been involved in groups which met monthly for group discussion over two years. They took the questionnaire after their meeting time.

Remarried Control Group

These subjects (6 males, 12 females) were to match charac teristics of the other two groups, so that they would have the same range in terms of age and socio-economic level. They were all caucasian and half of the group was Catholic, (approximately the same proportion as is found in this region of the country). They had not been in counseling before nor had they ever attended a support group for divorced or remarried persons. They were nominated for this group by colleagues of the researcher and were contacted by phone to be included in the research. Then, they completed the mailed questionnaire.

(Note: To be included in any of these groups the subject must now live in a family that has a child from a previous marriage.)

Procedure: All subjects completed the following questionnaire.

Instrument: Divorce Adjustment

Remarriage and Blended Family Questionnaire (C. Pino)
Follow-up Questionnaire to Marital Autopsy Research

Age_____   Age at Divorce_____
Number of Children_____   Age at Remarriage_____

A. Divorce Process

1. What were the reasons for divorce?
    a) Your reasons?
    b) Your ex spouse's reasons?
2. Who left the marriage first?
3. What were the grounds for divorce according to the divorce decree?
4. What did you learn from the divorce?
5. How did the divorce affect you?

B. Child Rearing

6. a) What is the type of contact with your ex spouse?
    b) How frequent is your contact with your ex spouse?
7. a) Does your ex spouse have custody or visitation rights?
    b) If there are visitation rights, how often are they?
    c) Are visitation rights given or shared with your ex spouse's family?
    d) IF so, how?
8. What is the extent of your responsibility for financial child rearing, recreational, religious aspects of bringing up your children?
    a) Of your ex-spouse?
    b) Of your new mate?
    c) Of significant others?
9. What is the amount of your responsibility for your stepchildren with regard to question number 8?
10. What is the amount of contact of your relatives with your stepchildren?

Remarriage

11. How did your children react to divorce?
12. How did your children react to remarriage?
13. How do your children relate to your stepchildren?
14. How do your children relate to their half-siblings?
15. How satisfied are you with your present marriage?
16. What types of conflicts were present in the first marriage?
17. What types of conflicts were present in the second marriage?
18. How stable, do you feel, is your second marriage?
19. What needs are there for improvement in the second marriage?
20. What do you feel is different about being a blended family?
21. How has it changed you?

    a) Your spouse?

22. What is the socio-economic level of your ex spouse?

    a) What is the socio-economic level of your present spouse?

23. What is the amount of support you receive from your relatives for past marriage? (5-extremely supportive to 1-extremely unsupportive)

    a) What is the amount of support you receive from your relatives for this marriage?

24. a) How much power to make decision do you feel you had in the first marriage on five point scale? (5-extreme power to 1-no power)

    b) How much power do you feel you have in second marriage on five point scale?

25. a) What nationality, religious denomination and age are you?

    b) Your spouse?

    c) Your ex spouse?

26. a) How much freedom do you feel you have in the second marriage on a scale of five points?

    b) How much freedom do you feel you had in the *first marriage* on a five point scale? (5-extreme freedom to 1-no freedom)

27. a) How much affection did you have in the first marriage on a five point scale?

    b) How much affection do you have in the second marriage on a five point scale? (5-extreme affection to 1-no affection)

28. Did you seek counseling prior to and/or after divorce?

29. a) What was the basis for choosing first spouse?

    b) What was the basis for choosing second spouse?

30. a) How did you prepare for first marriage?

    b) How did you prepare for second marriage?

31. What advice would you give to prospective remarrying individuals?

32. How did your background prepare you for marriage?

33. How did your background prepare you for rearing children?

34. a) What is the role of your in-laws in your life?

    b) What is the role of your ex-in-laws in your life?

35. a) What are your hopes for the future for your family?

    b) What are your fears for the future of your family?

36. How did "Link" (support group) or therapy help you?

Hypotheses

Adjustment problems of long-term therapy clients reflect heavily on their ability to cope with divorce and remarriage and concomitantly with their children's ability to cope with these changes (Pino, 1980). Thus it was hypothesized that: 1) the divorce treatment group would be likely to be rejected by their spouse (first spouse left the marriage); 2) the children of the treatment group subjects would be rated by their parents to have had more deleterious reaction to divorce and remarriage;[2] 3) that the treatment group would have lower mean perceived satisfaction, power, freedom, and affection level in terms of their first and second marriages.[3]

RESULTS AND DISCUSSION

The Divorce Process

The physical separation of partners is a crucial phase in the divorce process. The pain of this is great for both partners but is usually felt hardest by the person being rejected (Rice, 1977). Hypothesis number 1 tested that those under treatment would be more likely to be rejected. This follows from the fact that most of these clients were diagnosed neurotic and unable to give freely of themselves. Thus in terms of social exchange, it may be likely that the partners would tend to leave them more so than another less pathological group (Nye 1977). This can be seen in reactions to question number 2 on the questionnaire. Complex Chi square analysis was done to test this. This Chi Square value (2.4) p. > .05 failed to reach significance, thus rejecting this hypothesis. However, the value just missed significance at this level, indicating a significant trend in this direction. In fact, two thirds of the treatment group have been rejected by their first spouse while in the support group and control groups the ratio was approximately 50/50 of the spouses leaving compared to the subjects leaving the marriage. When we look at question number 1—the reason for leaving—it appears that in the treatment group the most common cause is spouse's infidelity (which accounted for nearly two-thirds of the subjects in this particular category). This particular pattern is quite distinct from the support group and control group subjects in which spouse's infidelity accounted for under one-third of those subjects while other reasons were more likely to be given by respondents of those two groups (e.g., drug or alcohol abuse, spousal desertion, incompatibility.)

Other questions in this section of the questionnaire looked at issue such as the legal grounds for the divorce. Most respondents in all three categories listed mental cruelty as a ground for the divorce. Questions 4 and 5 tended to elicit many different

91

types of responses by respondents in all three categories. However, the most frequently given response by those subjects in the treatment category were that they learned and had reacted to the divorce with some kind of depressive reaction. This was much less common reply to questions 4 or 5 by subjects in the support group and the control group. Thus, it appears that the treatment group seemed to be most painfully affected by the divorce compared to the other subjects; who are likely to give responses such as: "felt anxious," "worked harder," and "felt relieved."

Child-Rearing

Literature has been replete with questions about the length of time that it takes children to adjust to a divorce and to remarriage (Wallerstein & Kelly, 1980); (Kulka & Weingarten, 1979); (Heatherington, 1977); (Rahe, 1979). An effort to tap the parents' perceptions of the childrens' reactions were seen in questions 11 and 12 in the questionnaire. The first part of hypothesis two relates to question number 11—the effect of divorce on children. A complex Chi Square was computed and found to be non-significant. Thus, there were no significant differences between the three groups on their perceptions of the children's reactions to divorce. All groups had uniformly perceived their children as having negative reactions to the divorce; thus, rejecting this part of the hypothesis.

The second part of the hypothesis related to the childrens' reaction to remarriage. It was hypothesized that the treatment group would perceive their children as having a more difficult time in accepting the remarriage. Responses to question number 12 were categorized into positive and negative reactions and a Chi Square statistical analysis conducted which was found to be significant at the .05 level. Thus, the treatment group was found to perceive their children as having many more difficult reactions to remarriage as opposed to the other groups. In fact, over 80%

of this group had stated that their children reacted in a negative manner compared to 60% in the support group and 67% in the control group.

A number of items in this category in the questionnaire tended to indicate that the treatment group was experiencing more difficulty in blending the families. Question number 8 is particularly important to this finding. The extent of responsibility that the ex spouses took for their children was lower in the treatment group than in the support and control groups. This meant that the present spouses of those under treatment had to take more responsibility for the care of the stepchildren. For this group, this factor created a strain on the remarriage. Other items showed that there was less involvement of the family of the ex spouse for the children for the treatment group. The family of these subjects did, however, (in all three groups) provide an important service to the children and uniformly accepted the stepchildren, according to the subjects perception at least.[4]

One wonders about the quality of those interactions, however, since no item was given on the questionnaire to tap this. Children were likely to create more difficulties for the second marriage among the treatment group subjects as well (as seen in the reactions to question number 7—the types of conflict were present in the second marriage). Children tended to be reported as a source of conflict more commonly in the responses of the treatment group to this particular question. Also, alcoholism was also listed in response to the treatment subjects to the particular question. Perhaps alcoholism abuse would be seen by the spouse as a way to relieve the tension caused by disputes over the children. The other two groups were more likely to say that monetary problems or other types of minor adjustment problems were likely to be difficulties in their second marriages (if they reported having any difficulty).

All groups responded that their relationships to their

children were generally good (if they had much contact with them). All three groups reported low contact with stepchildren. This was due to the fact that all three groups had higher proportions of women and their stepchildren were usually awarded custody of their spouses' wives. When there was contact between their children and their stepchildren, the response of all three groups was generally positive. Likewise with question number 14—the relationship of children to half-siblings was generally good (in these cases where there were half-siblings).

Remarriage

The third section of the questionnaire attempted to assess the quality of life in the second marriage and compare it with the first marriage. Hypothesis number 3 asserted that the treatment group would be likely to derive less satisfaction in the second marriage and to perceive themselves as having lower levels of power, freedom and affection in the first and second marriages. This was measured by a five point rating scale on questionnaire items number 15, 24, 26 and 27. Significant t's (at the .05 level)[5] were found in: the lower satisfaction in the second marriage; lower power in the first marriage; in lower freedom in the first and second marriage; and in lower affection in the second marriage—in the treatment group when compared to the support and control groups. This was as expected in the hypothesis. However, contrary to that hypothesis, the treatment group was not significantly different in their perceptions of power in the second marriage as well as perceiving more affection in their first marriage compared with the other two groups. It was noted that all groups had made increases in power, freedom and affection in their perceptions of their second marriage when compared to their first. However, the treatment group perceived less of a gain in affection in going from their first to their second marriage. While their scale value for affection dimension was not significantly higher than the other two groups, the

94

treatment group did have a slightly higher value. It is as if they romanticized their first relationship when compared to the other two groups, and felt already disillusioned by their second marriage. Some light is shed on this particular phenomena from question number 29. The treatment group was more likely to give security (economic and practical help with raising the children, etc.) as the basis for the second marriage than the other two groups. Thus, the affection area may have been a less salient facet of family life for these subjects as compared to the other two groups. Therefore, it appears that their second marriages are more conflictual as seen in their lower scores on the questions and their responses to questions 17 and 18 (i.e., conflicts in marriage and needs for improvement in their second marriage). These subjects were more likely to: 1) relate to problems with the children as mentioned before, to report more symptoms, for instance, alcoholism and drug abuse on the part of their spouse as well as themselves; 2) to state that there were problems in blending the family, question number 20; 3) to perceive less parental support for both marriages as tested out in this particular hypothesis and found to be significant.[6] All three groups responded that in preparation for the second marriage, living together was a good idea. The majority of them had in fact done so. This poor parental support for both marriages has created difficulties for these individuals in trying to find satisfactory marital adjustment. Parental rejection in fact played a role in their own perceived difficulties in life as indicated in their responses to questions 32, and 33, i.e., "how did your family background prepare you for marriage" and "how did your family background prepare you for child rearing." In the majority of the respondents, the group under treatment reflected problems in conflictual and broken families. The other two groups were more liable to react to these questions by saying they had a close-knit family who prized the idea of marriage and that being members of a large family or babysitting experience or other positive experiences with children led them to be prepared to rear children. Parental rejection and neglect by contrast typified the reactions on the part of those in treatment. Moreover those in treatment had lower levels of contact and poorer perceptions of both in-laws and ex-in-laws compared to the support and control groups.

The Role of Treatment and Support Groups in Divorce and Re-marriage

Those in treatment were likely to answer the last question with a response indicating symptom remission as a treatment gain. They were likely to say they become less depressed, less anxious and got rid of certain undesirable habits or symptoms and gain more self control as responses to this item. Most of the outcome research in psychotherapy would indicate that these are typical responses (Strupp, 1969). Those in the support group were likely to answer this question with some kind of statement indicative of the fact that they had received personal affirmation by the group. For instance, the typical responses were: "the group made me feel good about myself;" "they shared their experiences with me which made me feel good;" "it lessened the isolation " "it helped me cope with my pains of divorce and the remarriage." It also formed friendships as many of the respondents in this group reported. This is clearly shown in the research of Foy & Kercher (1979). Thus, treatment and support groups serve slightly different, though overlapping functions. Those in treatment hope to alleviate undesirable symptoms and secondarily seek personal affirmation and support. Those in support groups are more likely to not have symptoms or at least deny them. They want the support from peers instead of professionals. They are likely to actively seek out friendships which may be already an indication of the higher levels of adjustment (Roschke, 1977).

Summary

While the questionnaire represents small samples of individuals in one locale, it does provide a description of some of the aspects of divorce adjustment, remarriage and reconstituting of a family. All of these processes appear more difficult in those undergoing treatment. These individuals were more likely to be labeled neurotic and had in fact a long history of difficulty which made them seek treatment in the first place, and after continuing contacts with mental health professionals. They were more likely to experience difficulties in affection, power, satisfaction and freedom in both their first and second marriages and had lower levels of family support for both marriages. All three groups tended to rely on relatives for some respite from children and stepchildren and found the process of living together prior to second marriage a helpful process in the blending of families. All three groups found that the children reacted in some upsetting fashion to divorce, but those under treatment found that their children reacted in a more negative manner to the remarriage than the other two groups. The low level of contact with the ex spouse in the treatment group place a very heavy burden on their new spouses. This led to additional problems in their second marriages which oftentimes encouraged them to continue treatment and provided greater dissatisfaction in their lives.

Treatment and support groups serve different, but somewhat overlapping functions. They both provide support but in different type ways. The control group was much like the other two groups in income and age. Most subjects were in fact in their mid-thirties particularly. However, they appear to be a particularly privileged group in that they sought no need for treatment or support group and as their responses indicated, they tended to have an easier time of adjustment in divorce and remarriage, and perhaps, were just generally better integrated individuals. That being the case, they probably were not a control group at all, but a comparison group of relatively "high functioning" individuals.

They did report their own problems in remarriage and blending families; e.g., conflicting loyalties of children towards their ex spouses, their mates and other minor adjustment complaints. Therefore, even with this group, some type of educational experience in preparation for remarriage and blending families (as described by Pino, 1980b; Nichols, 1977, etc.) may prove greatly beneficial.

While this is only a pilot project with many methodological problems, it may shed some light on the problems and promises of remarriage and the needs for therapy and education for the remarrying in the preparation of reconstituting a family.

CHAPTER FOOTNOTES

[2]Tested by Complex Chi-Square Analysis (Bruning & Kiniz, 1965).

[3]Tested by t-test of differences between group means (Bruning & Kiniz 1965).

[4]Chi Square = 7.7.

[5]Re: Marital satisfaction—t+13.2; Power—t=4.0; Freedom first marriage—t=6.0, Freedom in second marriage—t=11.7; Affection in first marriage—t=4.0; Affection in second marriage —t=8.0; Parental support for first marriage—t=5.0; Parental support second marriage—t=3.0.

[6]See footnote number 2.

CHAPTER VIII

PERSONALIZED MARRIAGE PREPARATION
AND FAMILY ENRICHMENT

A valuable resource developed by this author is *Personalized Marriage Preparation and Family Enrichment* published by United Educational Services, Inc.

Chapter 5 discusses Personalized Re-Marriage Preparation (P.R.P.) Program. These materials also could be utilized in ongoing family therapy with remarried couples and families. The exercise packet, in the appendix, and the various exercises which are described in chapters 4 and 5 are indeed a very useful adjunct to ongoing marriage and family therapy. Additionally, the use of contracting which was developed in family therapy and utilized in this enrichment work, applies very well to remarriage and premarriage counseling, as well. Therefore, these packages which were developed to do enrichment work can be easily used in a piecemeal or global basis to more systematically instrumented ongoing marital and family therapy.

Chapter 6 provides a merger plan which presents some questions regarding issues surrounding a merged family.

Chapters 5 and 6 are reprinted here.

Reprinted from Personalized Marriage Preparation and Family Enrichment

(CHAPTER V)

PERSONALIZED REMARRIAGE PREPARATION PROGRAM

Programs to prepare remarrying individuals have recently emerged. Walker, et al (1979) reviewed the literature in educational and treatment approaches to remarriage. Many of the articles she quoted dealt with the utilization of family therapy in child guidance to help in the process of blending families. Educational programs for remarriage will be exemplified by a model given by Nichols, (1979). His "problems in the second marriage" series include the following areas of concern: reactions to and residues from the first marriage and its ending on the part of both spouses in the second marriage. Also discussed are the children's discipline, finances, possessions, and inheritance matters.

The following is a description of an experiential workshop format for remarriage preparation—The Personalized Remarriage Preparation Program advised by the present author. The object of this non-denominational program is to focus on the needs of remarrying couples. The stress of step-children on the remarriages is well known and deserves special attention not usually provided by traditional marriage preparation programs. The present program is to extend innovative PMP Program to remarrying individuals by including exercises geared to access the effects of divorce and step-children on remarrying individuals. Some of the background for this is provided in an article published by Dr. Pino (1980) "The Marital Autopsy". This is a technique devised for divorce counseling that utilizes background information to review for remarrying individuals in a systematic way, their past likes in preparation for a new marriage. Such techniques are incorporated in the PRP approach. This is essentially an experientially-based type of learning that maximizes personal involvement

of the couple with theoretical input from mental health professionals on a team.

Test instruments to be utilized provide information to each couple and access their strengths and weaknesses pattern given from the Premarital Inventory (Bess Associates, 1969). The PMP exercises are reworded to fit the PRP workshop. The exercises have been coded to match the scales from the PMP. Ultimately each couple will write a marriage contract which will concretize their expectations for the marriage, just as given in the PMP approach. In fact, the schedule for PRP is much like PMP with few notable exceptions: on the first day, the background information is elicited from the couples on their relationships in the first marriages which is shared in the group discussion given in the afternoon (refer PMP schedule). On the second day, a "merger plan" is substituted on the 11:00 slot, (see Appendix for merger plan). Information from this particular exercise is referred to in a lecture given at 1:00 on dynamics of remarriage. Information from Vischer and Vischer's book, *The Step Families* (1980) is capsuled for this mini-lecture, and open sharing follows this. At 2:00, the rest of the afternoon follows as in the PMP Program. In fact, the PMP and PRP Programs are so compatible that the two laps can be run simultaneously given the availability of adjacent rooms for separate group discussion in which these groups are kept homogeneous i.e. "first marrieds", vs. remarrieds. Such an approach utilized the same team, (provided they have given expertise with remarriage, as with newlyweds), can easily be accommodated. This constitutes a savings in personnel costs, and allows certain lectures,(for instance,the overview of PMI,* and the conflict-management lecture), to be given to both groups at the same time. Sometimes, there are opportunities for an interchange between first marrieds and remarrieds that can be advantageous for both groups. First marrieds, for instance, usually wear "blinders to the fact divorce could occur ever" to them. The remarried individuals may have become jaundiced to the freshness of romance as seen in newlyweds. Nevertheless,

there are important inputs for the two groups that must be done separately, and this is particularly important. The first time we field tested the PRP Program we ran it simultaneously with a PMP. Besides a great age difference between the two groups (first marrieds averaged around 23 years, the remarrieds around age 36), the remarrying individuals tended to want to talk among themselves. They felt that many group discussions which included newlyweds would be counter-productive to them since they felt they had "been through the mill" already, as opposed to the inexperienced newlyweds. This could have been an isolated group experience but may, in fact, represent a common trend.

Future offerings of PRP should better access this trend. Current evaluation of the program is in progress. Again, as in the PMP Program, the same communication in conflict management questionnaires were given prior to and after the lab experience. From the post-meeting questionnaires, the responses had been very positive and edifying for three programs—PMP, PFE, and PRP. When asked particularly "what were the most helpful to you", respondents in all three programs felt that specific skills were advanced in Communication, Conflict Mangement, and in Contracting which led them to a high level of functioning. Most particularly, in the PRP group merger plan led to establishing a good set of guidelines for each specific couple to merge their family.

Reprinted from Personalized Marriage Preparation and Family Enrichment

(CHAPTER VI)

PRP MERGER PLAN

Preparation for reconstructing (or merging parts of two families) may involve several important issues. Below some questions regarding these issues are given. Please respond to them first.

(1) Housing

    a.   Where will you live?

    b.   What rooms, furniture, etc. will you need?

(2) Children

    a.   What arrangements are there for visitation (if it's applicable)?

    b.   How can the step-parent(s) be informed of the children's perception of their background?

    c.   What special preparation will individual children need?

    d.   How will they be disciplined?

(3) Finances

    a.   Have you worked out a budget? Discuss it?

    b.   What special financial needs will require savings in the next 10 years?

    c.   Have you made a will?

(4) Roles

    a.   What tasks (e.g. housework, financial, child care, recreational, etc.) will be performed by whom in the family?

(5) Recreation

    a.   How will each person be likely to spend their free time?

    b.   What family activities are likely to be arranged.

(6) Goals

    a.   What goals do you have as a family? What goals do you have as an individual? Is there any conflict between the two?

    b.   What blocks are there (that you can foresee) to these goals?

    c.   How can each family member help in accomplishing these goals.

CHILDREN

Each mate lists ten pet peeves about children and how they would handle it in their children.

Each mate will read their list and the couple will then decide who and how each situation will be handled. (Pick 2)

Process the exercise using the study questions:

1. What value conflicts arose in the exercise?

2. How were decisions made?

3. How do you feel about the decisions?

CHAPTER IX

SUMMARY AND POLICY ISSUES

The previous chapters constitute a state of the art of selected studies of divorce adjustment and divorce counseling. In surveying the literature and outline of the pertinent material in divorce adjustments, aspects of remarriage and reconstituted families have been discussed. Then, the results of three research studies on the presentation of the design of a fourth experiment currently in progress was reported. The first study was based on the utilization of the psychological autopsy to the demise of marriages. The marital autopsy is a tool of value for divorce research and divorce counseling. As a research tool the various stages of the divorce process were analyzed and appropriate measures to study the effects of each stage were given. In that particular study, several factors emerged related to the importance of independence after a divorce and the delineation of sources of support that help in the divorce adjustment process. Sex differences noted raise important issues for the differential experience of adjustment to divorce. The second study which utilizes a path model to study divorce adjustment was given in Chapter III. This paradigm combines life change theory with a behavioral resource exchange theory applied to study the divorce process. This research is currently in progress and results are not available to be discussed in the volume. One follow-up study conducted through the marital autopsy group looked at those individuals in that divorce population who were subsequently remarried and their experience in forming a reconstituted family. This research reported the differential effects of psychotherapy and various support groups selected from matched populations on a divorce process. It was concluded that both are extremely helpful in overlapping, but somewhat different sorts of ways, in helping the divorced person to come to terms with divorce and prepare for remarriage and the blending of families. Specific issues were outlined in this regard. A fourth study utilized imagery to probe the subjective experience of divorce. Thus, divorce imagery was studied in a population of Parents Without Partners to ascertain the importance of assertiveness in divorce adjustment. The typology of different divorce imageries emerged and assertiveness played an important role in divorce adjustment. However, some sex differences were noted in the distribution of types of divorce imagery coupled with the person's adjustment process. Both the marital autopsy and the divorce imagery processes were seen as important tools in divorce counseling. The examples of their use were given in previous chapters. Thus, in divorce, the importance of being able to review the marriage looms as critical to remarriage preparation and assertiveness seems essential to the immediate exigencies following separation. The field of divorce counseling and many other techniques have been reviewed in the last chapter as well.

Legal Issues: The majority of the states still adhere to an adversary model for divorce litigation. The adverse effects of this model as opposed to more recent development of "no-fault divorce" have been researched by many people, have been discussed by several people (e.g., Abel, 1973; Wright and Stetson, 1978; Blake, 1962 Rinestein, 1971). Spanier and Anderson (1979) point out in their research particular difficulties that arise in this adversary system. The majority of the respondents in Pennsylvania for instance, found difficulty with the legal system and "the data suggests that divorce statuses based on the adversary model encourage collusion and dishonesty." (page 612) Coozler (1980) has suggested mediation centers where trained marital counselors used mediation techniques to solve divorce litigation difficulties in a therapeutic fashion before an out-of-court settlement and subsequent divorce decree are granted. Sometimes unfortunate effects of this adversary model is the tendency for one of the parents to get custody and the other to become progressively less and less involved with the child. This issue has been taken to task by Freud, Goldstein, et al (1967). More recent researchers have taken the single parent custody issue to task. Galper (1978) documents the advocacy of a co-custodial relationship.

Single Parent Families: The increase in the single parent families in the United States has risen greatly over the 1970's. One source, C.O.F.O. (1979), found that in 1978, 19% of children below the age of 18 in the United States lived with one parent. In 1960, this figure was only 9%. In order to accommodate this growing proportion of single parent families, the National Task Force on Mental Health in 1978 made the following suggestions: 1) in order to accommodate working mothers, the extension of the school day or provision of other kinds of services for child care at an affordable rate of remuneration; 2) increase job sharing, flexible time and part-time work in order to allow custodial parent more time with their children; 3) flexible sick leave policies; and 4) respite care for children which would allow vacations for the single parent; 5) prevention training programs in the schools as suggesting parent education for single parents; 6) reciprocity between states to prohibit kidnapping of children. These are a few of the policy positions that might make life more livable for single parent families. The difficulties encumbered by single parents from schools have been outlined in Marriage and Divorce Today (January 12, 1981). They report a survey done by *Principal* magazine in which 75% of single parents polled were able to attend meetings without taking off from work which they found abusive. Child care while parents attended school activities was also a crucial issue (only 10% of the parents in the study indicated that child care was provided during parent activities). Few volumes and textbooks in the library deal with anything but two-parent families. Thus, this has ramifications towards creating negative self-image to children in single parent homes. The school was found seldom to take the lead in communicating with non-custodial parents. In 35% of the respondents had heard school personnel make "negative comments about single parent homes." "Nearly half of the participants heard school personnel mention broken homes or some other stereotype when speaking about single parent families." Thus difficulties with the school comprise a major source of concern for single parents.

Remarriage: In Chapter VII the issues regarding remarriage were discussed and survey conducted. One of the conclusions of the study was that marriage programs need to be instituted. A paucity of such programs exists today. One of the few groups invested in this process is the Step Family Association of America. However, as opposed to preparation, their impetus seems to be more in favor of working with families who have been together for some time. Such families have already encountered problems and are likely to have developed some problematic habits in interacting with one another. Thus more pro-active as opposed to reactive approaches need to be taken. One model has been presented by Messenger (1976); another has been devised by Pino (1980).

All these policy concerns and recommendations reflect current thinking among many social scientists. As our culture changes, they too will be soon outdated by the time legislation may be passed and implemented. The lag time required to make a change in our country's inherent culture is particularly felt in the area of divorce and remarriage. This document does not mean, however, that the prospects are bleak. Indeed the horizons look a good deal more positive than is outlined here.

APPENDIX A

EGO FUNCTIONS ASSESSMENT (Sharp & Bellack, 1978)

EGO FUNCTION	COMPONENTS
1. Reality testing	a. Distinction between inner and outer stimuli b. Accuracy of perception c. Reflective awareness and inner reality testing
2. Judgment	a. Anticipation of consequences b. Manifestation of this anticipation in behavior c. Emotional appropriateness of this anticipation
3. Sense of reality	a. extent of derealization b. extent of depersonalization c. self-identity and self-esteem d. clarity of boundaries between self and world
4. Regulations and control of drives, affect and impulses	a. directions of impulse expression b. effectiveness of delay mechanisms
5. Object Relations	a. degree and kind of relatedness b. primitivity (narcissistic attachment or symbiotic object choices) versus maturity c. degree to which others are perceived independently of one-

EGO FUNCTION	COMPONENTS
	self
	d. object consistency
6. Thought processes	a. memory, concentration and attention
	b. ability to conceptualize
	c. primary-secondary process
7. Adaptive regression in the service of the ego (ARISE)	a. regressive relaxation of dignitive acuity
	b. new configurations
8. Defensive functioning	a. weakness or obtrusiveness of defenses
	b. success and failure of defenses
9. Stimulus barrier	a threshold for stimuli
	b. effectiveness of management of excessive stimulus input
10. Autonomous functioning	a. degree of freedom from impairment of primary autonomy apparatuses
	b. degree of freedom from impairment of secondary autonomy
11. Synthetic-integrative functioning	a. degree of reconciliation of incongruities
	b. degree of active relating together of events
12. Mastery-competence	a. competence: how well subject actually performs in relation to his capacity to interact with

and actively master and affect
his environment
b. the subjective role, or subject's
feelings of competence with
respect to actively mastering
and affecting his environment
c. the degree of discrepancy between component (a) and component (b) (i.e., between actual
competence and sense of competence).

Divorce Outcome - Adult adjustment Scale Vailliant (1978) - 31 items in
the areas of career, social, psychological and physical health. Ratings made
by two clinicians after interviewing each client.

RATING SCALES

1. Adult Adjustment Scale (a rating from 0 to 32)

Taking the entire twenty-five-year period (from college graduation to 1967) into account, one point was assigned for each of the following thirty-two items that was true. A score of less than 7 defined the Best Outcomes; a score of 14 or more defined the Worst Outcomes.

I. Career

   a. Failure to receive steady promotion or increasing responsibility, if possible, every five years since graduation.

   b. Not listed in *Who's Who in America* or *American Men of Science*.

   c. Earned income is less than $40,000 (unless in teaching, clergy, or responsible public service or quasi-charitable work).

   d. Earned income is less than $20,000 (1967).

   e. Occupational success does not clearly surpass father's (income, responsibility, occupational status).

   f. Occupational success clearly does not equal father's.

* g. Has not actively participated over the years in extracurricular public service activities.

   h. However prestigious in the eyes of others, his job either is not one that he really wants for himself, or over the years it has failed to match his realistic ambitions.

*Rater agreement for each item was eighty-five to one hundred percent, except for items marked with an asterisk, where agreement was seventy-five to eighty-five percent.

II. Social Health

   a. Failed to achieve ten years or more of marriage (without separation) or failed to express overt satisfaction with that marriage on two or more occasions after the first year. (Eventual divorce did not affect this item.)

   b. Divorced, separated, or single. (Exclude widowers.)

   c. Never wanted to have or adopt children. (Ignore this item if he is single due to external cause - e.g., Catholic clergy.)

d. One-third or more of children are markedly underperforming scholastically, delinquent, or getting psychiatric care. (Subsequent data analysis showed that this question would have been useful in 1975, but in 1967, when it was asked, it correlated with nothing.)

e. Maintained no contact with surviving family of origin, except by duty or necessity.

f. Regularly stated that he has less than usual interest in or fewer than average number of close friends. (Subjective evidence.)

* g. Not regularly a member of at least one social club and evidence from less than two occasions that he has more than one close friend. (Objective evidence.)

h. No regular pasttime or athletic activity that involves others (family members do not count).

N.B. Items a, b, c, i, g, and h were used to separate the Friendly from the Lonely men.

III. Psychological Health

* a. For more than half of years described, did not use full allotted vacation time or spent it at home doing chores or on dutiful visits to relatives.

b. Explicit statement that subject had missed something by being too calm, unruffled, controlled, or unemotional (at two points in time). (Like Item 11-d, this item was not signficantly correlated with overall adjustment.)

* c. Failure to express satisfaction with job on three or more occasions and once in the past three years.

d. Expressed explicit dissatisfaction with job at three points in time and once in past three years, or had changed occupational field once or job three times since age thirty without evidence of concomitant improvement in personal satisfaction or success.

e. Evidence of detrimental (interferes with health, work or personal relations at home) use of alcohol, or use of sedative or stimulant drugs weekly for more than three years, or more than six ounces of hard liquor a day for three years, or use of tranquilizers for more than a year.

f. Ever hospitalized because of mental breakdown, alcohol misuse, or "physical" illness without evidence of somatic pathology.

g. Evidence on more than two occasions that he is chronically depressed, dissatisfied with the course of his life, or evidence that he is consistently labeled by himself or others as being emotionally ill.

h. Has sought psychiatric help for more than ten visits.

IV. Physical Health

a. One hospitalization or serious accident since college (Item not significantly correlated with overall adjustment.)

b. More than two operations and/or serious accidents since college (battle wounds excluded). (Item not significantly correlated with overall adjustment.)

c. Two hospitalizations since college (excluding those due to surgery, trauma, or physical checkup).

d. Own estimate of general health since college expressed in less than the most favorable available terms on more than one-fourth of occasions.

e. On the average, misses two or more workdays a year due to illness.

f. On the average, misses five or more workdays a year due to illness.

g. Afflicted with chronic illness (requiring medical care) that significantly limits activity or more than a month of work lost consecutively due to illness.

h. Regularly takes prescription medicine; several patent medicines; or seeks medical attention for minor medical conditions (headaches, sinusitis, allergy, skin conditions, etc.).

117

2. Childhood Environment Scale (a rating from 0 to 20)

In the 1970s, research associates who were blind to the fate of the men after their sophomore year, but who were not blind to more recent theories of child development, especially Erikson's, rated the men on the adequacy of their childhoods on a 20-point scale. The only data made available to the judges were (a) the psychiatrist's and family worker's notes on the boy's reports of his home life, (b) the parents' description of their relationship with the boy, and (c) a developmental and medical history obtained by the family worker from the parents. The family worker intereviewed the parents in their homes.

A score of under 6 defined the Loveless and of 14 or more defined the Lucky. The 20-point scale was as follows:

a. **Infant/Childhood Problems:** Feeding problems, cried a great deal, dissocial, other noted problems (e.g., phobias) - no points. An average not particularly problem-filled childhood - 1 point. No known problems to age ten, normally social and "good-natured" - 2 points.

b. **Childhood Health:** Severe or prolonged illness, or physical disability - no points. A childhood with minor illnesses but no severe childhood diseases - 1 point. Consistent good health - 2 points.

c. **Home Atmosphere:** An uncongenial home with lack of family cohesiveness with early maternal absences, separated parents, many moves or financial hardship which affected family life - no points. An average home or little information - 1 point. Close enjoyable relationship with at least one thing together in a sharing atmosphere; few moves and financial stability - 2 points.

d. **Mother-Child Relationship:** A distant, hostile, or absent mother; one who blamed others (i.e., nurses, teachers, etc.) for her wrong methods of upbringing; a mother who seemed either overly punitive and demanding, or over-protective and/or seductive - no points. Lack of definite information or an apparently average relationship - 1 point. A warm mother who encouraged autonomy and esteem - 2 points.

e. **Father-Child Relationship:** An absent, distant, hostile, or overly punitive father; one with unrealistic expectations - no points. Lack of definite information or an apparently average relationship - 1 point. A warm father who encouraged positive autonomy, helped to develop his son's self-esteem, and who participated in activities of mutual interest - 2 points.

f. **Sibling Relationship:** Severe rivalry and destructive relationship where one sibling consistently undermined the other, or no siblings - no points. Lack of information - 1 point. Close enjoyable relationship with at least one sibling - 2 points.

g. **High School Adjustment:** Marked social problems - no points. "Average" social adjustment but no competitive sports - 1 point. Social success with participation in competitive sports - 2 points.

h. **Global Impression** (This was the judge's overall impression of the childhood environment based on the available data): Impression of generally negative, non-nurturing environment - no points. Predominant impression neutral - 3 points. A positive childhood which included warm sustaining relationships and an environment conducive to developing autonomy, self-esteem and initiative (one the judges themselves would have wanted) - 6 points.

Score values range from 0 - 20 points.

Source: G. Vailliant. *Adaptation to Life*. LH6. Brown: Boston, 1979.

THE IMPACT OF LIFE CHANGES

1. Order Number of Occurrences indicate how many times in the past year each of the events has occurred.
2. Multiply the number under Score Value by the number of occurrences of each event and place the answer under Your Score.
3. Add the figures under Your Score to find your total for the past year.

LIFE EVENT	Number of Occurrences	Scale Value	Your Score
Death of spouse	_____	100	_____
Divorce	_____	73	_____
Marital separation	_____	55	_____
Detention in jail or other institution	_____	63	_____
Death of a close family member	_____	63	_____
Major personal injury or illness	_____	53	_____
Marriage	_____	50	_____
Being fired at work	_____	47	_____
Marital reconciliation with mate	_____	45	_____
Retirement from work	_____	45	_____
Major change in the health or behavior of a family member	_____	44	_____
Pregnancy	_____	40	_____
Sexual difficulties	_____	39	_____
Gaining a new family member (e.g., through birth, adoption, oldster moving in, etc.)	_____	39	_____
Major business readjustment (e.g., merger, reorganization, bankruptcy, etc.)	_____	39	_____
Major change in financial state (e.g., a lot worse off or a lot better off than usual)	_____	39	_____
Death of a close friend	_____	37	_____
Changing to a different line of work	_____	36	_____
Major change in the number of arguments with spouse (e.g., either a lot more or a lot less than usual regarding childrearing, personal habits, etc.)	_____	35	_____

LIFE EVENT	Number of Occurrences	Scale Value	Your Score
Taking on a mortgage greater than $10,000 (e.g., purchasing a home, business, etc.)	_____	31	_____
Foreclosure on a mortgage or loan	_____	30	_____
Major change in responsibilities at work (e.g., promotion, demotion, lateral transfer)	_____	29	_____
Son or daughter leaving home (e.g., marriage, attending college, etc.)	_____	29	_____
In-law troubles	_____	29	_____
Outstanding personal achievement	_____	28	_____
Wife beginning or ceasing work outside home	_____	26	_____
Beginning or ceasing formal schooling	_____	26	_____
Major change in living conditions (e.g., building a new home, remodeling, deterioration of home or neighborhood)	_____	25	_____
Revision of personal habits (dress, manners, associations, etc.)	_____	24	_____
Troubles with boss	_____	23	_____
Major change in working hours or conditions	_____	20	_____
Change in residence	_____	20	_____
Changing to a new school	_____	20	_____
Major change in usual type or amount of recreation	_____	19	_____
Major change in church activities (e.g., a lot more or a lot less than usual)	_____	19	_____
Major change in social activities (e.g., clubs, dancing, movies, visiting, etc.)	_____	18	_____
Taking on a mortgage or loan less than $10,000 (e.g., purchasing a car, TV, etc.)	_____	17	_____
Major change in sleeping habits (a lot more or a lot less sleep, or change in part of day when asleep	_____	16	_____
Major change in number of family get-togethers (e.g., a lot more or a lot less than usual)	_____	15	_____

LIFE EVENT	Number of Occurrences	Scale Value	Your Score
Major change in eating habits (a lot more or a lot less food intake, or very different meal hours or surroundings)	_____	15	_____
Vacation	_____	13	_____
Christmas	_____	12	_____
Minor violations of the law (e.g., traffic tickets, jaywalking, disturbing the peace, etc.)	_____	11	_____

THIS IS YOUR TOTAL LIFE CHANGE SCORE
FOR THE PAST YEAR   _____

If you score less than 150 points, you have one chance in three of getting a serious illness in the next two years; if you score between 150 and 300, your chances are 50-50. If you score more than 300 points, your chance of serious illness is almost 90 percent.

Source: Thomas E. Holmes, M.D., Department of Psychiatry, University of Washington.

APPENDIX B

TABLE II

PSYCHIATRIC OUTPATIENT DATA

	Range	Mean	SD
1. Chronological Age			
Married Males	21-62	38.5	6.8
Unmarried Males	18-57	34.6	6.9
Recently Divorced Males	22-48	36.0	5.8
Married Females	20-61	38.1	5.9
Unmarried Females	18-60	28.6	6.3
Recently Divorced Females	22-48	36.0	5.8
2. Length of Marriage			
Married Males	1-40	12.5	8.7
Recently Divorced Males	1-24	12.4	8.1
Married Females	1-40	8.1	6.8
Recently Divorced Females	1-24	11.4	7.9
3. Childhood Environment			
Married Males	2-18	12.5	5.2
Unmarried Males	2-16	9.0	5.1
Recently Divorced Males	3-18	10.1	5.1
Married Females	3-18	12.0	5.3
Unmarried Females	2-17	10.0	5.2
Recently Divorced Females	4-18	11.2	5.3
4. Number of years living independently before marriage			
Married Males	0-10	4.0	1.8
Recently Divorced Males	0-7	2.4	1.3
Married Females	0-5	2.0	.7
Recently Divorced Females	0-4	1.1	.5

	Range	Mean	SD
5. Life Change Units			
Married Males	94-260	135	14.0
Unmarried Males	91-160	117	19.5
Recently Divorced Males	138-413	253	22.0
Married Females	84-147	127	25.1
Unmarried Females	63-133	113	26.0
Recently Divorced Females	131-390	240	20.1
6. Resources			
Unmarried males	1-5	2.5	.48
Recently Divorced Males	1-4	2.1	.60
Unmarried Females	1-5	3.0	.50
Recently Divorced Females	2-5	2.5	.50

APPENDIX C

TABLE III

REASON FOR DIVORCE: DISSOLUTION

Stage in Percent

	MALES	FEMALES
Spouse's Infidelity	% = 40	% = 36
	N = 10	N = 9
Self Infidelity	% = 12	% = 4
	N = 3	N = 1
Verbal Abuse	% = 20	% = 20
	N = 5	N = 5
Spouse's Alcoholism or Drug Problem	% = 8	% = 16
	N = 2	N = 4
Financial Problems	% = 4	% = 4
	N = 1	N = 1
Physical Abuse	% = 0	% = 8
	N = 0	N = 2
Fear of Commitment to Spouse	% = 12	% = 8
	N = 3	N = 2
In-law Problems	% = 4	% = 4
	N = 1	N = 1

TABLE IV

COPING MECHANISM: Pre-Terminal

Stage in Percent

	MALES	FEMALES
Narcissism	% = 48	% = 44
	N = 12	N = 11
Aggression	% = 12	% = 32
	N = 3	N = 8
Object Attachment	% = 8	% = 4
	N = 2	N = 1
Overwork	% = 32	% = 20
	N = 8	N = 5

TABLE V

FAMILY ADJUSTMENT: Course of Marriage

Stage in Percent

	MALES	FEMALES
Unstable - Unsatisfactory	% = 16	% = 40
	N = 4	N = 10
Stable - Unsatisfactory	% = 60	% = 40
	N = 15	N = 10
Unstable - Satisfactory	% = 24	% = 25
	N = 6	N = 5
Stable - Satisfactory	% = 0	% = 0
	N = 0	N = 0

References *

Backiel, L., Daily, S. and Washburne, C.K. (Eds.). *Women in Transition.* New York: Charles Scribner's Sons, 1975.

Bardwick, J.M. and Douvan, E. Ambivalence: The Socialization of Women. In Judith M. Bardwick (Ed.) *Readings on the Psychology of Women.* New York: Harper & Row Publishers, 1972, 52-62.

Barrera Merz, Isaura. The Role of Student Characteristics in Making Assessment Decisions About Hispanic Students Referred to Special Education. Ph.D. Dissertation, State University of New York at Buffalo, 1985.

Bem, S.L. The Measurement of Psychological Androgyny. *Journal of Consulting and Clinical Psychology,* 1974, *42,* 155-162.

Bem, S. On the Utility of Alternative Procedures for Assessing Psychological Androgyny. *Journal of Consulting and Clinical Psychology,* 1977, *45,* 196-205.

Bernard, Jessie. *The Future of Marriage.* New York: Bantam Books, 1972.

Broverman, I.K., Broverman, D.M., Clarkson, F.E., Rosengrantz, P.S., and Vogel, S.R. Sex-Role Stereotypes and Clinical Judgments of Mental Health. *Journal of Consulting and Clinical Psychology,* 1970, *34,* 1-7.

Burlin, F. Sex-Role Stereotyping: Occupational Aspirations of Female High School Students. *The School Counselor,* 1976, 24(2), 102-108.

* Compiled by Judith Vogtli. Personality Attributions Ascribed to Divorced Mothers, Ph.D., Dissertation, SUNY at Buffalo, 1987.

Chesler, P. *Women and Madness.* New York: Avon Books, 1972.

Constantinople, A. Masculinity-Feminity: An Exception to a Famous Dictum. *Psychological Bulletin,* 1973, *80,* 389-407.

Darley, S. Big Time Careers for the Little Women: A Dual Role Dilemma. *Journal of Social Issues,* 1976, *32,* 85-98.

DeCrow, D. *Sexist Justice.* New York: Vintage Books, 1975.

Deutsch, Morton, *The Resolution of Conflict: Constructive and Destructive Processes.* Yale University Press, 1973.

Elstein, A.S. and Bordage, G. The Psychology of Clinical Reasoning.In Stone, G., Cohen, F. and Adler, N. (Eds.) *Health Psychology.* Washington, D.C.: Jossey-Bass, 1974.

Erickson, Erik H. *Identity: Youth and Crises.* New York: W.W. Norton, 1968.

Fischer, J.L. Childfree Relationships: Mothers Living Apart from Their Children. Paper presented at the Groves Conference on Marriage and the Family, The Poconos, Pennsylvania, 1981.

Fischer, J.L. and Cardea, J.M. Mothers Living Apart from Their Children: A Study in Stress and Copying. *Alternative Lifestyles,* *4*(2), 1981, 218-27.

Freedman, J.L., Carlsmith, M.C., and Sears, D.O. *Social Psychology.* New Jersy: Prentice-Hall, Inc., 1974.

Frieze, I.H., Parsons, J.E., Johnson, P.B., Ruble, D.N. and Zellman, G.L. *Women and Sex Roles.* New York: Norton and Company, 1978.

Gardner, R.A. *The Boys and Girls Book About Divorce.* New York: Bantam Books, 1976.

Glick, P. and Carter, H. *Marriage and Divorce.* Cambridge: Harvard University Press, 1970.

Goldstein, J., Freud, A. and Solmit, A.J. *Beyond the Best Interests of the Child.* New York: The Free Press, 1973.

Goode, W. *The Family.* Englewood Cliffs: Prentice Hall, 1964.

Hammond, K.R. The Cognitive Conflict Paradigm. In L. Rappoport and D.A. Summers (Eds.). *Human Judgment and Social Interaction.* New York: Holt, Rinehart and Winston, 1973.

Hammond, K.R. (Ed.) *Judgment and Decisions in Public Policy Formation.* Boulder: Westview Press, 1978.

Hammond, K.R. and Joyce, C.R.B. (Eds.) *Psychoactive Drugs and Social Judgement: Theory and Research.* New York: John Wiley & Sons, 1975.

Hammond, K.R., McClelland, G.H., and Mumpower, J. *Human Judgment and Decision Making.* New York: Praeger Publishers, 1980.

Hammond, K.R., Wascoe, N.E. *Realization of Brunswik's Representative Design.* San Francisco: Jossey-Bass Inc., Publishers, 1980.

Hansen, L.S. and Rapoza, R.S. (Eds.). *Career Development and Counseling of Women.* Springfield, Illinois: Charles C. Thomas, 1978.

Herrerias, Catalina. Noncustodial Mothers: A Study of Self-Concept and Social Interactions. Dissertation, 1984.

Herrerias, Catalina. Noncustodial Mothers: Loving is Leaving. Paper presented at the Annual Meeting of the Society for the Study of Social Problems, San Antonio, Texas, 1984.

Hetherington, Cox & Cox, 1976. From Rawlings, E.I. and Carter, D.K. Divorced Women. *The Counseling Psychologist,* 1979, *8*(1), 27-28.

Isenhart, M.A. Divorced Women: A Comparison of Two Groups Who Have Retained or Relinquished Custody of Their Children. Dissertation Abstracts International, 1980, 5628-A.

Jung, Carl G. *Man and His Symbols.* New York: Dell Publishing Co., 1977.

Kanowitz, L. *Women and the Law.* Albuquerque: University of New Mexico Press, 1972.

Karpicke, S. Perceived and Real Sex Differences in College Students' Career Planning. *Journal of Counseling Psychology,* 1980, 27(3), 240-245.

Keller, F.O. The Childless Mother: An Evaluation of Deviancy as a Concept in Contemporary Culture. Ph.D. Dissertation, California School of Professional Psychology, San Francisco, 1975. University Microfilm International, Ann Arbor, Michigan, 1981.

Kessler, S. "Building Skills in Adjustment Groups," *Journal of Divorce,* Vol. 2, 1978.

Kessler, S. *Creative Conflict Resolution: Mediation.* Atlanta: National Institute of Professional Training, 1978.

Krantzler, J. *Creative Divorce.* New York: Evans, 1974.

Lipman-Blumen, J. and Leavitt, H.J. Vicarious and Direct Achievement Patterns in Adulthood. in L.S. Hansen & R.S. Rapoza (Eds.), *Career Development and Counseling of Women.* Springfield, Illinois: Charles C. Thomas, 1978.

Miller, 1976, p. 93. From Rawlings, E.I. and Carter, D.T. Divorced Women. *The Counseling Psychologist,* 1979, 8(1), 27-28.

Newell, A. Judgment and its representation: An Introduction in, B. Kleinmuntz (Ed.). *Formal Representation of Human Judgment,* New York: John Wiley & Sons, 1968.

Orthner, D.K., Brown, J. and Ferguson, D. Single-parent fatherhood: An emerging family lifestyle. *Family Coordinator,* 1976, 25, 429-437.

Otto, H.A. and Otto R., 1976. From Rawlings, E.I. and Carter, D.K. Divorced Women. *The Counseling Psychologist,* 1979, 8(1), 27-28.

Parkes, 1972. From Rawlings, E.I. and Carter, D.K. Divorced Women. *The Counseling Psychologist,* 1979, 8(1), 27-28.

Paskowicz, P. *Absentee Mothers.* New York: Allanheld/Universe, 1982.

Pearson, J. "The Denver custody mediation project," in R. Day and H. Raschke (Eds.) Divorce Newsletter Update. Brookings: South Dakota State University.

Petrinovich, L. Probabilistic functionalism: A concept of research method. *American Psychologist,* 1979, 34:5, 373-390.

Pino, C.J. *Divorce, Remarriage, and Blended Families: Divorce Counseling and Research Prospectives.* Palo Alto: R & E Research Associates, Inc., 1982.

Rapoza, R.S. and Blocher, D.H. A Comparative Study of Academic Self-Estimates, Academic Values, and Academic Aspirations of Adolescent Males and Females. In L.S. Hansen & R.S. Rapoza (Eds.). *Career Development and Counseling Women.* Springfield: Illinois, Charles C. Thomas, 1978.

Rappoport, L. and Summers, D.A. (Eds.) *Human Judgment and Social Interaction.* New York: Holt, Rinehart and Winston, Inc., 1973.

Rawlings, E.I. and Carter, D.K. Divorced Women. *The Counseling Psychologist,* 1979, *8*(1), 27-28.

Ricci, I. *Mom's House, Dad's House.* New York: Macmillan Publishing Co., Inc., 1980.

Ross, S.C. *The Rights of Women.* New York: Avon Books, 1973.

Rothert, M.G. The likelihood of patient adherence to a medical regiment: Comparison of patients' and physicians' judgment. Dissertation, Michigan State University at East Lansing, 1980.

Rothert, M.G. Physicians' and patients' judgments of compliance with a hypertensive regiment. Medical Decision Making, 1982, 2, 179-195.

Ware, C. *Sharing Parenthood After Divorce.* New York: The Viking Press, 1982.

Weisstein, N. Psychology Constructs the Female, or the Fantasy Life of the Male Psychologist. In Babcox, D. and Belfin, M. (Eds.) *Liberation Now.* New York: Del Publishing Co., 1971, 267-286.

Whitely, Counseling Psychology in the Year 2000 A.D. *Counseling Psychologist, 8*(4), 3.

Wiggins, J.S. *Personality and Prediction Principles of Personality Assessment.* Massachusetts: Addison-Wesley Publishing Company, 1973.

Woolf, V. *A Room of One's Own.* New York: Harcourt, Brace and World, 62, 1957.

Yanico, B.J. Sex-Role Self Concept and Attitudes Related to Occupational Daydreams and Future Fantasies of College Women. *Journal of Vocational Behavior, 19,* 1981, 290-301.

Yanico, B.J., Hardin, S.I. Sex-Role Self Concept and Persistence in a Traditional vs. Nontraditional College Major for Women. *Journal of Vocational Behavior,* 1981, *18,* 219-227.

BIBLIOGRAPHY

Abel, R.L. "Lawbooks and Books About the Law." *Stanford Law Review* 26:1973 (175-222).

Ahsen, A. *Eidetic Psychotherapy*. NY: Brandon House, 1976.

Bach, G. "Creative Exists," in *Women in Therapy*, G. Franks and M. Butle, NY: Brunner/Mazel, 1973.

Bane, M. "Marital Disruption and the Lives of Children" in Levinger and Moles. *Divorce & Separation*. NY: Basic Books, 1979.

Bergler, E. *Divorce Won't Help*, NY: Harper & Row, 1948.

Bernard, J. *Remarriage: A Study in Marriage*, NY: Dryden, 1956.

Bernard, J. "No New but New Ideas," in *Divorce and After*. D. Bohannan.

Bernard, Jr. *The Future of Marriage*, NY: Antheum, 1974.

Bernard, J. "Note on Changing Life Style," 1970-1974. *Journal of Marriage and the Family*, Aug. 1975, 582-593.

Berrelson, B. and G. Steiner, *Human Behavior* 1977. NY: Harcourt, 1964.

Bischof, L. *Interpreting Personality Theories*, 2nd ed. NY: Harper & Row, 1970.

Bitterman, C. "The Multi-Marriage Family." *Social Casework*. 49: 218-221, 1968.

Blake, N.M. *The Road to Reno*. NY: MacMillan, 1962.

Bloom, B.S., White, S., A.S. Lan "Marital Disruptions As a Stressful Life Event," *In Clevenger and D. Noles.*

Bohannan, D. p. ed. *Divorce and After,* NY: Doubleday, 1974.

Bohannan, P. In J. Kaplan's *Comprehensive Handbook of Psychiatry.* Philadelphia: Saunders, 1974.

Bowerman, C. & D. Irish, "Some Relationships of September Children to their Parents." *Marriage and Family Living,* 24, May 1962, pp. 113-121.

Brandwein, R., Brown, C., and Fox, E. "Women and Children Last" *Journal of Marriage and Family.* 1974, No. 4.

Briscoe, H. "Depression in Divorce." *Archives of General Psychiatry.* April 1975, No. 34.

Brunning, J. and B. Z. Kintz. *Computational Handbook of Statistics.* Glenview, IL: Scott-Foresman, 1966.

Bryant, L. "Filing Patterns and Transition," *Journal of Marriage and the Family.*

Burchinal, J. "Characteristic of Adolescents from Unbroken, Broken, Reconstructed Families in American Families" *Journal of Marriage and the Family,* Vol. 261, Feb. 1964, 44-51.

Cautela, J. "Covert Conditioning." In A. Jacobs and I. Sachs. *Psychology of Private Events.* NY: Academic Press, 1971.

Chevlin, A. "Work Life and Marital Dissolution" In *Divorce and Separation,* G. Levinger and D. Noles.

C.O.F.O. (Coalition of Family Organization) Newsletter, Vol. II. No. 3, Summer/Fall, 1979.

Coozler, O. J. *Structural Mediation in Divorce Settlements.* Lexington, Mass.: Lexington Books, 1978.

Duberman, L. "Step-kin Relationships" *Journal of Marriage and the Family* 35, May, 1973, pp. 287-292.

DuVall, E. *Family Development*, 4th ed. Philadelphia: Lippincott 1971.

Fast, J. and A. Cain "The Step-Parent Role" *American Journal of Orthopsychotherapy*, 1966, pp. 485-491.

Fischer, E. *Divorce: The New Freedom* NY: Harper & Row 1974

Foy, J. and Kitcher, K. "The Impact of Catholic Support Groups on Post-Divorce Adjustment." *Marriage and Divorce Today* Vol. 5, No. 14, Nov. 19, 1979.

Framo, J. "Divorce Therapy" address at American Association of Marriage and Family Therapy, NY, 1974.

Furstenberg, F. "Premarital Pregnancy and Marital Instability," In *Divorce and Separation*, G. Levenger and D. Noles.

Galper, L. *Co-Custody* Philadelphia: Runners Press, 1978.

Gardner, R. *Psychotherapy with Children of Divorce*, NY: Aaronson, 1978.

Gardner, R. *The Boys' and Girls' Book about Divorce*, NY: Aaronson, 1970.

Gardner, R. *Explaining Divorce to Children*, NY: Signet, 1969.

Garek, E. "Note on Remarriage" In *Marriage & Family Today*, February 24, 1980.

Garfield, R. "The Decision to Remarry," Address at American Association of Marriage and Family Therapy, *Washington, D.C., 1979.*

Glenn, N. & C. Weaver, "Mental Happiness of Remarried, Divorced Persons" *Journal of Marriage and the Family*, May 1977.

Glick, P. "Marrying, Divorcing and Living Together Therapy" *Population Report*, Washington, DC: October 1976.

Glick, P. and H. Carter, *Marriage and Divorce*, Cambridge, Mass.:

135

Harvard University Press, 1970.

Goldman, J. and J. Coane "Family Therapy after the Divorce: Developing a Strategy" *Family Process.* 16:357-362.

Goldstein, H. "Reconstituted Families: The Second Marriage and Its Children." *Psychiatric Quarterly.* 48:433-440, 1974.

Goldstein, A. *Community and Living Skills.* NY: Pergamon, 1976

Goode, W. *After Divorce* Glencoe, IL: Free Press, 1956.

Goode, W. *The Family,* Englewood Cliffs, NJ: Prentice Hall, 1964.

Gould, R. "Phases of Adult Life," American Journal of Psychiatry, 1973.

Gretemen, J. *Divorce Program.* Sioux City, IA: Catholic Charities, 1979.

Gunderson, E. *Life Stress and Illness.* Springfield, IL: Charles Thomas, 1974.

Gurin, P., Feld, P. and Veroff, J. *Americans View Their Mental Health,* NY: Basic Books, 1960.

Gurman, A. "Research on Marital and Family Therapy." *Handbook of Psychotherapy and Behavior Change,* 2nd ed., A. Garfield and A. Bergon, ed. NY: Wiley, 1978.

Harren, V.R. Kass, H. Tinsley, and J. Moreland. "Influence of Sex Role, Attitudes and Cognitive Styles on Career Decision Making." *Journal of Counseling Psychology,* 1978, Vol. 25, No. 5, 390-398.

Hetherington, M. "Effects of Parental Absence on the Personality Development in Adolescent Daughters." *Developmental Psychology* 7, 313-326, 1972.

Hetherington, M. "Divorced Fathers," *Family Coordinator,* Vol. 25, No. 4, October, 1976.

Herman, K. "Divorce — A Grief Process," *Perspective in Psychological Care* Vol. XII, no. 3, 1974.

Herson, M. and A. Bellach. "Social Skills Training for Chronic Psychiatric Patients." *Comprehensive Psychiatry*, 1976, 17, 559-580.

Hillman, K. "Marital Instability and its Relation to Education, Income and Occupation" in R. Winch, et al *Selected Studies in Marriage and the Family*, NY: Holt, Rinehart and Winston, 1962.

Holmes, P., Rahe, R., "Life Change and Illness," In R. Moos, *Human Adaptation*, NY: Pergamon, 1976.

Hunt, M. *The World of the Formerly Married.* NY: McGraw-Hill, 1961.

Hunt, N. F. *The Divorce Experience* NY: McGraw Hill, 1977.

Jackson, R. and Lederer, W. *The Mirages of Marriage*, NY: Basic Books, 1969.

Jacobson, O. "Stepfamilies: Myths and Realities" *Social Work* May, 1979, pp. 202-307.

Johnson, S., *First Person Singular*, NY: Lippincott, 1977.

Kaplan, F. "A Structural Family Therapy Approach to Single Parent Families." *Family Process*, Summer, 1980.

Kerlinger, F.M. and Pedhanguer, E.J. *Multiple Regression in Behavior Research.* NY: Holt, Rinehart and Winston.

Kessler, S. *The American Way of Divorce*, Chicago: Nelson-Hall, 1975.

Kessler, S. "Building Skills in Adjustment Groups" *Journal of Divorce*, Vol. 2, No. 1978.

Korman, E. and R. Stewart "Group Program for Children of Divorce." Buffalo: Child and Adolescent Psychiatric Clinic, 1980.

Krantzler, J. *Creative Divorce.* NY: Evans, 1974.

Kulka, R. and H. Weingarten, "The Long Term Effects of Parental Divorce in Children." Address at American Sociological Association: Boston, 1979.

Lazarus, A. "Assertiveness Training with Depressed Patients." *Behavior, Research and Therapy.* Vol. 6, 1968.

Lazarus, R. *Psychological Stress and Coping Process.* NY: McGraw Hill, 1966.

Leslie, W. *The Family in Social Context.* 3rd ed., NY: Oxford Press, 1976.

Levinger, G. "Marital Cohesiveness of the Break" In *Divorce & Separation,* G. Levinger and D. Noles, ed.

Levinger, G. and D. Noles, ed. *Divorce and Separation,* NY: Basic Books, 1979.

Lindemann, E., "Symptomology and Management of Acute Grief," *American Journal of Psychiatry,* 1944, No. 101, pp. 141-148.

Maynes, M. and Sheresky, N. *Uncoupling,* NY: Dell, 1972.

Marriage and Divorce Today - Vol. 1, 5 No. 1, Aug. 20, 1979.

Marriage and Divorce Today - *Vol. 6, No. 23, Jan. 12, 1981.*

McCormick, M. "Stepfathers: What the Literature Reveals" *Palo Alto, CA: Western Behavioral Research Inst., 1974.*

McCubbin, H., B. Dahl, D. Benson and M. Robertson, "Coping Responses of Families Adapting to War Induced Prolonged Separations," Journal of Marriage and Family. 1977, 38, August, 461-471.

McDermott, E. "Parent Divorce in Early Childhood." In R. Moos *Human Adaptation.* Lexington: Heath, 1976.

McNemar, R. *Psychological Statistics.* NY: Wiley, 1961.

Messinger, L. "Remarriage Between Divorced People with Children from Previous Marriages," *Marriage and Family Therapy*, Oct., 1979, Vol. 2, pp. 183-200.

Morrison, J. "Successful Grieving: Changing Personal Constructs Through Mental Imagery." *Journal of Mental Imagery.* 1977, 2, 63-68.

Moos, R., *Human Adaptation*, Lexington, Heath, 1976.

Mueller, C.H. and Pope "Marital Instability, A Study of Generations" In *Marriage and the Family*, 1977, Vol. 83-93.

Mowatt, M. "Psychotherapy for Step-Fathers and their Wives." *Psychotherapy, Theory, Research, and Practice.* 9:328-331 1972.

New York State Governor's Conference on the Family (Proceedings) Albany: New York Governor's Office, 1980.

Nichols, W. "Divorce and Remarriage." *Journal of Divorce,* Vol. 1, Winter 1977, pp. 153-163.

Nye, B. *Role Structure and Family Analysis.* Beverly Hills: Sage, 1977.

Nye, I. and S. McLaughlin, "Role Competence and Marital Satisfaction" H.I. Nye, *Role Structure and Family Analysis,* San Francisco: Sage, 1977.

Nye, J. "Child Adjustment in Divorced and Unbroken Homes." *Marriage and Family Living,* No. 19, Nov. 1957, 11357-61.

Olson, R. *Emotional Flooding.* NY: Behavioral Science, 1976.

Perls, F. *Gestalt Therapy.* Glencoe, IL: Grove Press, 1951.

Pino, C. "Divorce Eidetic, Post-Divorce Coping, and Assertiveness." *Journal of Counseling and Psychotherapy,* (Ch. 5), 1981.

Pino, C. *Personalized Marriage Preparation and Family Enrichment,* East Aurora, NY: United Educational Services, 1986.

Pino, C. "Marital Autopsy." *Journal of Divorce*. Fall, 1980, 6.

Pino, C. "The Coping With Separation Inventory - Revised." Buffalo: Unpublished, 1979.

Raschke, H. "The Role of Social Participation in Post Separation and Post Divorce Adjustment." *Journal of Divorce* Vol. 1, Winter 1977, pp. 130-141.

Rathus, S. "A 30-Item Schedule for Assessing Assertive Behavior" *Behavior Therapy*. 1976, Vol. 7

Reichard, R., Livson, R. and Peterson, W. *Aging and Personality* New York: Wiley, 1962.

Rheinstein, M. *Marriage, Divorce Stability and the Law*. Chicago University Press, 1971.

Rice, D. "Psychotherapeutic Treatment of Narcissistic Injury in Marriage, Separation and Divorce." *Journal of Divorce*, Vol. 1, Winter 1977.

Rogers, C., *Becoming Partners*, NY: Delacort, 1972.

Roman, E. and A. Trice *The Sociology of Psychotherapy* NY: Aronson, 1975.

Satir, V. *Conjoint Family Therapy*. Palo Alto: Science and Behavior Books, 1964.

Scanzoni, J. "A Historical Perspective on Husband-Wife Bargaining Power and Marital Dissolution." In *Divorce and Separation*, D. Levinger and D. Noles.

Schneidnam, E. *Essays in Self-Destruction*. NY: Science House, 1967.

Schorr, J. *Watching the Movies in Your Head*. NY: International Med., 1976.

Seligman, M. *Learned Helplessness*. Chicago: Freeman, 1974.

Sharp, W. and L. Bellak "Ego Function Assessment of the

Psychoanalytic Process," *Psychoanalytic Quarterly*, 1978, No. 1, 52-62.

Sheehy, G. *Passages*. NY: Bantam, 1976.

Sheffner, J. and R. Suarez "A Post Divorce Clinic." *American Journal of Psychiatry*, 1975.

Siegel, G. *The Grief Process*. Nashville: Abrigdon, 1976.

Singer, L. "Divorce and Single Life." *Journal of Sex and Marriage*. September 1975, No. 1.

Spanier, G. and E. Anderson, "The Impact of the Legal System on Adjustment to Marital Separation." *Journal of Marriage and Family Therapy*, Vol. 41, No. 3, Aug., 1979 (605-614)

Stampfl, T. and T. Levis. "Essentials of Implosive Therapy." *Journal of Abnormal Psychology*. 1967, 72, 496-503.

Steinzor, B. *When Parents Divorce*. NY: Pantheon, 1969.

Stetson, D. and G. Wright, "The Effects on Divorce in American States," *Journal of Marriage and the Family*, A. 1975, 537-545.

Stewart, J. *A Manual for the Beginning Experience*, Ft. Worth, North Texas: Family Life Department, 1976.

Strupp, H. *Patient's View Their Psychotherapy*, NY: Aronson, 1975.

Tennant, A. and Andrews, D. "Pathological Quality of Life Stress in Neurosis." *Archives of General Psychiatry*. June 1978.

Toffler, A. "Omnigany," *Psychology Today*, April 1978.

Vailliant, G. *Adaptation to Life*, NY: Random House, 1978.

Vischer, E. and J. Vischer, *Step Families*, NY: Brunner/Mazel, 1979.

Walker, L. et al, "An updated Biography of the Remarried, the Living Together, and Their Children." *Family Process*, June, 1979, pp. 193-212.

Waller, W. *The Old Love and The New*, Carbondale, IL: Southern Illinois University Press, 1967.

Wallerstein, J. and S. Kelly "California's Children and Divorce" *Psychology Today*, January, 1980.

Weisman, A. *The Psychological Autopsy*, NY: Behavioral Press, 1968.

Weiss, R. *Marital Separation*, NY: Basic Books, 1974.

Weiss, R., "The Emotional Impact of Marital Separation." *Journal of Social Issues*, 1976, 32, 135-146.

Wolpe, J. and A. Lazarus. *Behavior Therapy*. NY: Pergamon, 1966.

Woman in Transition, Inc., *Women in Transition — A Premarital Handbook on Separation and Divorce*. NY: Scribners, 1975.

Wright, G. C. and A. M. Stetson, "The Impact of No-Fault Divorce Law Reform on the Divorce in American States." *Journal of Marriage and Family*, No. 40, August 1978 (587-580).

NOTES

NOTES

Printed in the United States
875800002B

9 780595 168583